MIMESIS
INTERNATIONAL

ATMOSPHERIC SPACES
n. 15

What is an "Atmosphere"?

According to an aesthetic, phenomenological and ontological view, such a notion can be understood as a sensorial and affective quality widespread in space. It is the particular tone that determines the way one experiences her surroundings.

Air, ambiance, aura, climate, environment, genius loci, milieu, mood, numinous, lived space, Stimmung, but also Umwelt, ki, aida, Zwischen, in-between – all these words are names hiding, in fact, the founding idea of atmospheres: a vague ens or power, without visible and discrete boundaries, which we find around us and, resonating in our lived body, even involves us.

Studying atmospheres means, thus, a parte subjecti, to analyse (above all) the range of unintentional or involuntary experiences and, in particular, those experiences which emotionally "tonalise" our everyday life. A parte objecti, it means however to learn how atmospheres are intentionally (e.g. artistically, politically, socially, etc.) produced and how we can critically evaluate them, thus avoiding being easily manipulated by such feelings.

Atmospheric Spaces is a new book series whose aim is to become a point of reference for a community that works together on this philosophical and transdisciplinary subject and for all those whose research, more broadly, is involved in the so-called "affective turn" of the Social Sciences and Humanities.

Rudolf Gassenhuber and Robert J. Kozljanič

IN SEARCH OF LOST LIVELINESS

Nature, Dominance, Sense of Heart – the Long Way to Friendship with Nature

A Dialogue in Letters

The text was first published in German in 2019 by Ziel Verlag Augsburg. The expanded and revised English version is published with the kind permission of Ziel Verlag.

Translated by Richard Falzmann

© 2024 – MIMESIS INTERNATIONAL
www.mimesisinternational.com
e-mail: info@mimesisinternational.com

Book series: *Atmospheric Spaces*, n. 15

Isbn: 9788869774782

© MIM Edizioni Srl
P.I. C.F. 0241937030

CONTENTS

1.
Friendship with the Great or the Small Nature?

Rudolf Gaßenhuber   February 11, 2016

Dear Dr Kozljanič

I have just finished reading your inspiring book "Friendship with Nature"
and would like to send you a small review and ask a question.

Kind regards

Rudolf Gaßenhuber

Robert J. Kozljanič   February 11, 2016

Dear Mr Gaßenhuber

I am, of course, interested in your review and your question!

As I have noted, you also are a member of the "Society of New
Phenomenology". On April 8, 9, 10, 2016 I will speak at the conference on
religious experience on the topic of "Nature-aesthetical Contemplation and
Secularized Religious Experience of Nature Today." Could probably be an
opportunity for discussion ...

Best regards

Robert J. Kozljanič

Rudolf Gaßenhuber												February 11, 2016

Dear Mr Kozljanič

Thank you for your friendly invitation. […] I read your book "Friendship with Nature" with great interest and benefit. As I understand your text, you are in search of the great nature, of landscapes, demons and visions of elementary souls and primal grounds. Nature is believed to show itself, to impress and to give us a striking answer to the important questions of life. Your text is rather not in quest of the small nature, the unspectacular, the garden, the flea that does not die, the animal that encounters a human. You make, one could say, a selection among possible accesses to nature. And your interest is rather directed towards an evincing divinity, which can be experienced in particular occurrences. The exceptional seems to be the essential characteristic of such an access: ecstatic enthusiasm, the exaltation of phenomena to the allegory of God, and to the epiphany of the Olympians, breakthroughs, visions and demons.

Apart from that you are practically not talking about relations and totemism; and not at all about a tangible friendship between man and animal as in the case of Androcles. Recorded from Roman times by the antiquary Aulus Gellius, the story of Androcles tells about the friendship between a human and a lion. Presumably the story was filigreed and dramatized but will probably have a true core.

Androcles, an escaped slave, relieves a wild lion in Africa from a big thorn in a purulent wound. Both become friends and live together for years. – As fate wants it, they are separated, the escaped slave gets caught and unknowingly they finally meet one another in the Circus Maximus. For his flight, the escaped slave is to be punished to being ripped to pieces by the lion. The lion, however, recognizes his former friend and both come and meet warmly and joyfully. The spectators and the emperor are moved and both are freed in the end[1].

---

1   This story can be found at: https://en.wikipedia.org/wiki/Androcles

Androclus and the Lion,
a Roman tale, illustrated by
John Dickson Batten
around 1910

Your experience with the dormouse, however[2], goes in a different direction and has appealed to me particularly. I would like to go into this experience in greater detail and ask you a question.

You pass the night in a cave and dream of dangerously approaching mice and rats. At last a dormouse awakens you. It is nosing around in your rucksack, and you drive it away. In the morning the little animal is still there, you realize its purely trusting presence, and you criticize yourself for your defensive and anxious attitude: "So this chappy held up a mirror to me ..."

What happened here? I am not talking about fear, I mean the feeling of sympathy by saying: "this chappy". What was your reaction on this feeling? For it shows a certain devotion/opening of your heart, a response, the beginning of an encounter and possible attachment.

If, at all, nature speaks to us, it is here where we can find it, I think. Thus my question is: What was your reaction, when the chappy gave you this

---

2   Robert Josef Kozljanič: Freundschaft mit der Natur – Naturphilosophische Praxis und Tiefenökologie, Klein Jasedow 2008, pp. 51-52.

trusting presence? And when the night flew by and you were allowed to look into his dark button eyes?

The way I see it is, it was here when you were the closest to the topic of your book "Friendship with Nature". What you describe is a change from anxiety to confidence, a shift from fight to togetherness. If the occidental, dominant spirit is to become friends with nature, would not this be a model for such a change? It would be a way of an inner and outer friendship, a way that rather inhabits the world than affirming itself in it. Confidence has dissipated anxiousness. This is not obvious. The success feeds on friendship with basic trust and it adds to it.

View from the Klausen Cave

The dormouse is a little example for the transition from unfamiliarity and anxiousness towards social interaction with another being. For hunters and gatherers even all action is social action (Tim Ingold). It would then be the great key for a world, where the differences of spirit and world, nature and culture, technology and communication in today's hostile and conflicting form do no longer exist.

This condition of ONE world as an all-comprising social area, even lies underneath the layer which you describe in your book as the oldest, archaic level of the history of mankind – and traces of it remained a vital certainty at all times across all levels. One day or other mankind has lost its key for its home – but dormice and the like are to be found again and again.

Kind regards

R. G.

Robert J. Kozljanič   February 12, 2016

Dear Mr Gaßenhuber

Your lines and your characteristic of my book and my concept affect me in various ways:

A) For you see and describe quite clearly the fact and the way I aim for the 'exceptional' of a "great nature" – as well as for the epiphanic potential of it; including all advantages and disadvantages.

B) For you rightly point to the fact that the 'small nature' – the tender-quotidian, the trusting confidence, well, nature in general as it can show itself to be so deep and amicable in small creatures and gestures and close relationships – is neglected (thereby?) by me. Your suggestions at the dormouse and also at Androcles (behind whom the 'great nature' is shining forth indeed, for his story is pretty unusual) are touching me deeply. A similar image, a similar experience is on my mind: When at dusk (after long sitting and waiting on a tree for instance) a shy deer or – as I once experienced – a shy doe enters the clearing: What a deep and 'wonderful' experience it is! It is of the kind that a free creature openly shows itself – as such and as nature, as a free being showing and unfolding itself. Those who could ever watch it at close range how graciously deer or stag move, how cautious, graceful and naturally involved – and then pausing with a lifted foreleg and attentively erect eavesdroppers ; those who have ever seen it, will never forget it. If an amicable relationship develops in reality from such (repeated) experiences between man and animal, a trusted relationship, something like the deer coming out in the dusk knowing well that I am not far away – how 'Androclestic' wonderful ...

Deer

C) For you point to another very central aspect with your hint at the key concept of the totemistic-social dimension; an aspect I have been 'chewing' for a long time, but which I have not integrated enough (for time reasons) into the overall concept; when taking a closer look, it has been already mentioned, but only to a short and marginal extent. You wrote: "The dormouse is a little example for the transition from unfamiliarity and anxiousness towards social interaction with another creature. It would then be the great key for a world, where the differences of spirit and world, nature and culture, technology and communication in today's hostile and conflicting form do no longer exist. This condition of ONE world as an all-comprising social area, even lies underneath the layer which you describe in your book as the oldest, archaic level of the history of mankind – and traces of it remained a vital certainty at all times across all levels. One day or other mankind has lost its key for its home – but dormice and the like are to be found again and again".

How right you are: This level is underneath (or also within?) the archaic layer; and by all means across all other levels. And: this level seems to be the great key. It enables a deep, pacified feeling of being home and living at home ...

And here a question I have comes into play: How can we impart our contemporaries an awareness of the world actually being an all-comprising social area? How can it be found out? And above all, how can it be lived? In a time and in a society that conditions its members systematically and from an early age on that the non-human world is silent and therefore has no voice? In a world that is far too loud and numbing – and in which those who open their deeper and finer senses only have to suffer? How can those countless voices of all those big and small beings get a hearing in this culture of silencing (Derrick Jensen)? I think: Eichendorff's generally romantic-aesthetic as-though-experience ("It was as though the sky had silently kissed the earth") is not sufficient – here it is not enough to retreat into the garden and into tranquillity. Here Ludwig Klages' dictum applies: "The trees rustle, but they only speak to those whose soul once rode with the wind". And in my opinion, this is the reason why the archaic and totemistic hunter and gatherer cultures are shamanistic, why their main access to their ancestors and protective spirits of the clan is shamanistic visionary, and the reason why they communicate in a visionary way with natural beings. And this is why I put such a strong emphasis on the exceptional, ecstatic, visionary boundary experience of nature. (Maybe too much so?) I think, we need boundary experiences and crises in order to throw us out of our civilizing comfort zone, to burst (or to melt) the encrustations, to break out from the solely human and also solely social cages. At least, I have not been able to discover a better alternative, which could result from the personal point of view respectively a narrow personal view.

Out of the comfort room

In my lecture "Vision and Responsibility – From Self-Fulfilment to Nature-Fulfilment and Back"[3] I tried to work out once again this point more clearly. The jury is still out here. Maybe even not the first, initial word! Therefore I appreciate your clear and rich thoughts experienced in nature very much: for they affect central aspects and doubts, which are not at all unfamiliar to me, and which I would like to discuss in a more comprehensive and relevant way ...

Thank you very much!

And warm regards!

R. J. K.

---

3   Given at the international symposium "Into the wild. Growing inside, Acting outside!" of the Arbeitsgemeinschaft Jugendfreizeitstätten Sachsen e.V. of December 13, 2013

2

ECSTASY, EVERYDAY LIFE AND THE OPENING OF THE SENSE OF HEART

Rudolf Gaßenhuber   February 15, 2016

Dear Mr Kozljanič

I was very pleased to receive your overly kind and copious letter. Your frank readiness to think about the 'small nature' surprised me and makes me willing to reconsider my scepticism towards divine vocations and predestinations.

You are mentioning escapes, the transgression of limits, even bursts that would be necessary, let's just say, to be able to free the contemporary ego from its mental prison. It is true, the modern containment of nature requires a partition towards the soulful character of nature. Only through this partition, i.e. objectivisation modern objects come into existence. Formerly existing beings have become mere matter and function. Mother Earth becomes a resource.

Boniface fells the Oak of Donar, splits boards from it and builds a small chapel of wood out of them, where the new Christian God finds his home

Through this gesture Boniface condenses the symbolic exodus of divinity from nature, the transformation of nature into a natural resource and the construction of a new space of adoration and contemplation. Now God dwells in a house that was ascribed to him by man. Hence nature can be materialized successively. Its protection as a creation of God is much weaker than its identity with divinity was before. In your words: Nature is silenced, hardly makes itself heard.

This partition is a long process, which made a huge leap with agriculture and animal husbandry and has reached a temporary peak today with the programming of creatures in biotechnology and so forth.

How can this partition be reopened or overcome? I would like to answer in two ways. First with my own current answer, through a heart-opening and then by trying to approach your topic of visions.

A) *Silence*

A heart-opening would be the way back to the world. Boniface leaves his wooden church and starts to comprehend what sort of inner and outer destruction he has done. Donar's punishment did not fail to materialize. However, it did not consist in lightning and tempest but in man's world deprivation. Once there was a splendid tree, its rustling, its vivacity, its integrity, its ability of dialogue, its protective canopy. Tons of rage and grief accompany this discernment.

This is the way into a relationship with other beings: Empathy, compassion, the eye of the heart as you say so lovely in your speech. I would suggest for this purpose to reuse the more appropriate term, which has almost become extinct: the "sense of heart". With this sensory organ we owe a sense of our own, some sort of a passive sense of touch for the emotions of the soul of other beings; we are touched and appealed.

Boundary experiences and the recourse to unusual phenomena in this context are, as for me, under suspicion to take part in the deadening of the sense of heart and the enhancement of self-reference. At this point I would like to entrust to you the following presentation: "Stimmungen, Balancen, Grundkräfte – ein Modell des Heilseins"[1].

In the first part I outline a model of psychosocial health, the second part deals with our topic starting from page 18 on. There it says: "In the course of history, our attachment to nature has strongly diminished through a growing alienation. Modern man does no longer feel as part of nature – something like man among animals – but rather as its opponent. A direct feeling of being appealed by nature is declining." Subsequently three ways of the alienation from nature are outlined:

The distancing from natural phenomena, the charging of the mundane, and the modern technical access to the world.

B) *Storm*

What is Klages' point here: "The trees rustle, but they only speak to those whose soul once rode with the wind"? The important word here is "once". The storm is a necessary transition, the voices of the trees can only be perceived later. I could agree here very well. As a therapist I experienced a lot of heart-openings, which is always connected with a lot of emotionality and above all with waves of grief. But also diseases, blows of fate, and other critical boundary experiences can reopen the sense of heart. Thus such a "storm" may often be the case. (Yet, there are many people who live from early childhood on in such a modus vivendi.)

Here we must ask ourselves indeed about the very meaning of such boundary experiences, visions, and paranormal perceptions: Are they possible catalysts and door openers, or is this assumption even our main access to nature, the path to the primal ground of the divine? As far as the first estimation is concerned, we seem to be of the same opinion, as for the second one, I am not certain. You write "that the archaic and totemistic hunter-gatherers have a shamanistic culture, their main access to their ancestors and protective spirits of the clan is a shamanist and visionary one." I would doubt that. The ancestors and the spirits were they not a part of life, part of the scenery, part of daily life in the first place? And the shamans were they not healers and conciliators in case of insulting the spirits, i.e. they were helpers in a crisis and not mediators people needed

---

1   http://www.kontingenztherapie.de/artikel/theorie/Heilsein/Heilsein.pdf

permanently?[2] I write: "Ask ourselves indeed", for it is the assessment of vision and revelation that kindles the whole history of an authoritarian understanding of religion, of exclusive religious experience as the legitimation of priesthood. This notion of religion is bound to hierarchic societies, I think, and is out of harmony with the generally egalitarian societies of hunters and gatherers.

When putting the topic of dominance aside, we can ask what can be the nature of visions, and what is their relation to the sense of heart? When Boniface, taken as a parable, kneels down in his chapel and has a vision, what is it then? You have mentioned this already and emphasized the relevance of sensual experience. The inner attitude comes in addition; real closeness to nature is not a goal in Mosaic religions, believers rather worship the creator of nature. Visions and revelations of this cultural area rather aim at a different direction: Not at nature but behind nature, not at the counterpart but at obedience. Trenchantly asked: So when raised in a dualistic worldview, to which extent can an individual experience nature at all? Won't he stay almost forever and completely separated by his sort of boarding?

C) *After the storm*

As you can see, I am struggling. I will not live up to your expectations here. You do search in the nature as well in a conscious attitude. You describe an encounter with nature when freely unfolding as a feeling of happiness; the shy character is esteemed and respected. The encounter is even more touching when resulting in an encounter and trust. I happened to find a nice Androcles encounter with a dolphin yesterday: youtube.com/watch?v=Z2iw5-B88KA . This time a dolphin seeks help from a diver. A fishing line has tangled up around a pectoral fin and seemingly cut in. The diver helps the dolphin in several smaller steps even using a knife. The video clearly shows the dolphin's active searching for help and mutual understanding.

---

2   Here I refer to Tim Ingold: Hunting and Gathering as Ways of Perceiving the Environment, in: Ingold, T., The Perception of the Environment, London & New York 2000, pp. 40–60. Tim Ingold succeeds in describing the non-dualistic worldview of hunters and gatherers in an impressive and convincing way.

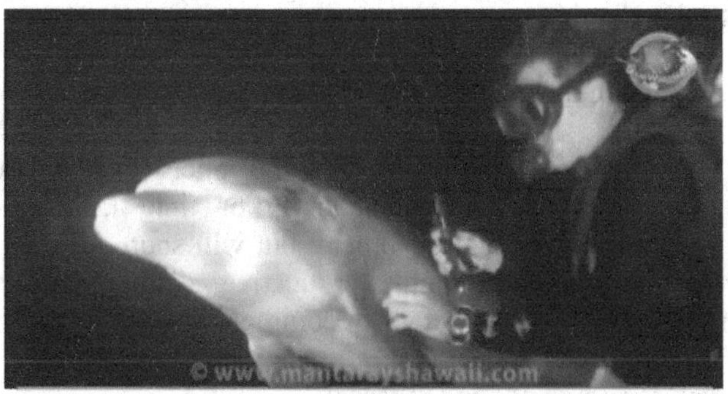

Dolphin and diver

And finally here is my story of happiness: When in a mood of open addressability, I can experience a connection with any occurrence. I experience a feeling of togetherness, for instance when walking along the river. I can feel the slow drift of it, and I feel a pleasant drag in my body (which is explained as a kinaesthetic perception). My body goes along with the drift and feels a pleasant drag especially at a certain part of the Danube – like balm. I sway with the gulls in the water.

A child passing by hand in hand with his father shouts: "So many pigeons!" I can feel his enthusiasm. But his father does not stop. I look up – a small flock of pigeons flies up to the roofs, I fly with them.

I look into human faces like into windows: The first glance, a first resonance. You look inside and often you see chaos, tristesse, strain, and sometimes satisfaction. Some windows are complex and complicated. I experience the grief and the laughter of a child, and the couple starts smiling ... I have to close my mind in order to avoid faltering indeed ...

Actually I think, the sense of heart is so crucial. It opens up a new world. Nietzsche once said correspondingly: "Those who have a 'why' will find their 'how'." It is the will, the determination, the sense that captures your imagination and removes all doubts – a life in a storm. I would argue: "Those who know the 'how' don't ask for a 'why'." Those who have once experienced the net of togetherness, the creature among creatures knows that questioning a "why" does not make any sense.

Kind regards

R. G.

Robert J. Kozljanič   February 18, 2016

Dear Mr Gaßenhuber

Thank you for your extremely revealing and concise thoughts, references concerning experiences, and metaphors. For time reasons I cannot answer more extensively at the moment, but will soon do, for I consider the conversation with you highly productive, dialogic and profound. Fascinating. Something like that is not common, at least for me.

Thank you for now and kind regards!

Robert J. Kozljanič   March 13, 2016

Dear Mr Gaßenhuber

Finally I have found the time to answer you. It is a long letter. But you have addressed and triggered so many important points ...

Especially inspiring were the (deeply symbolic) images you depicted and elaborated in your e-mail: Silence, storm, after the storm ...

Your Boniface parable expresses exactly what I feel. By the way in my two-volume work "The Spirit of a Place" I portrayed this development (also in architectural history): The destruction of divine powers and appearances in the world and in nature by Christian missionary work together with the Christian formation of a holy interior space (church), which is opened towards the supernatural and a world-overcoming transcendence. At the same time I asked the question about the significance of the fundamental man and place relationship: In which case can we speak about friendship relations and integrative ones and when about relations of transformation and superstructure.

I was quite impressed how exactly you looked at the Klages quote! In fact: The trees speak after the storm – to the one who once drove through the storm. I have to confess this (perhaps important) nuance escaped my attention. Your reading and your interpretation was better than mine here – and thereby you made something accessible to me. Thank you.

At the same time the big question remains indeed, as you wrote. I cannot justify it more specifically here, but I am of the (equally ethnologically proven) opinion that the egalitarian and archaic, the orally transmitting early societies that were based on subsistence agriculture and not strictly on the division of labour had their main access to nature in their visionary (mythical-animistic) way. The formation of authoritarian, hierarchic priesthood (based on inequality, oppression, and ideological brainwashing) occurred roughly speaking during and after the so-called "Axial Age" (Jaspers) hence with the emergence of a separate caste of priests and scholars; when people started regulating, monopolizing, canonizing, and fixing visionary experiences in written form. Thus Mosaic religions for instance systematically blocked or forbade many visionary channels and accesses: Great parts of nature and death manticism, obsessional trance and daimonic visions. Just the voice of God and angelophanies loyal to party principles were allowed; the same applies to prophetic visions and a divine afflatus; everything else tended to be marginalized and called diabolical ...

Your words concerning the opening of the sense of heart equally make me quite sensitive. It is a lovely and appropriate term, and also your assumption that boundary experiences rather deaden the sense of heart than opening it. I would like to consider this point more exactly; with a view at your multifaceted and colourful, far-reaching and profound presentation: "Stimmungen, Balancen, Grundkräfte – ein Modell des Heilseins". The three fundamental forces which you expose in such a clear and creative manner – body, sociality, and relationship with nature (resp. confidence in one's own body, one's own family/society and the world/nature) – are three important pillars of emotional and mediating security within our world and entirely in line with my philosophical tradition, the philosophy of life ("Lebensphilosophie"). However, I have never encountered such a concise compilation there, only now in your case. Thank you again for this.

I think that the two summarizing points show a slightly generalizing formulation:

1) "A good deal of the problems of humanity does not result from politico-economic reasons, but from our tremendous distance towards nature."

2) "The solution of this problem remains uncertain, but it won't be a 'just carry on' in the present direction."[3] The missing criticism of power you postulate in my concept of visionaries (in which, to my mind, you unjustly assume a priestly hierarchy mechanism): Here I would call for your criticism, for the criticism of power in my opinion as in yours is a central point resp. an important fundamental attitude and competence. And I am grateful if you point out to possible blind spots; for with particular reference to the criticism of power, everybody has his own blind spots; even the 'greatest' masters (like Marx or Nietzsche); in terms of the criticism of power I still consider myself a learner, albeit a more advanced learner hopefully ...

But don't get me wrong: The enormous distance towards nature – as you call it – is a greater problem actually, I would see it likewise. But it should be pursued together with a criticism of power, civilization, and capitalism. Derrick Jensen is a certain role model in that respect.

As for the enormous distance towards nature you mention three reasons:
"(A) Distancing from the phenomena of nature",
"(B) Charching of mundane life",
"(C) modern technical access to the world."

Ad *A) Distancing from the phenomena of nature*

You mention the following points: The process of civilization as a course of degradation of sensibility and of deep experience of nature; a growing alienation from nature and world; the sinister evolution from worldliness and the immanence of nature towards an escalation of intellectualistic concepts and narcissism and a proliferating absence of world and nature.

Ad *C) Modern technical access to the world*

To my mind point C seems to be closely intertwined with the civilisation process, in this context you invoke genetic engineering as an example for

---

3   Cf. the ingenious Georg Christoph Lichtenberg aphorism: "Admittedly, I cannot say whether it will be better if it is different; but I can say this much, it has to be different to be good."

the mechanization process. You write: "'Nature as a toolbox', this is voiced here repeatedly quite innocuously without noticeable shame. The weekly newspaper DIE ZEIT summarizes it like this: The goal of scientists is to 'tinker creatures genetically in a way that they do the job they are needed for'[4]. In a playful manner nature is declared on the quiet to 'Legoland' (analogy to Disneyland) here, where everybody can help himself." – I think that as far as these points are concerned we agree indeed.

Ad *B) Charging of mundane life*

This point seems to be crucial for you – and equally for me though maybe in a different weighting. "Emotional charging of mundane life" as you call it: But how about introducing the subjective genitive and objective genitive for a differentiation of this expression? Namely: On the one hand the mundane appears as artificially (metaphysically/ideologically) enhanced and charged (quasi from the exterior) and functions either as an instrumentalized object or an object to be instrumentalized; on the other hand the mundane itself enhances and charges something – out of daily life; therefore it appears as a subject of an autonomous or distinctive momentum of enhancement and charge. In a way that the enhancement and charge unfolds automatically, quasi naturally in daily life but overlaps the latter, because the enhancement interrupts and alters the merely mundane life in its calm and relaxed state or its salvaging-salvaged routine or in its grey, boring, and monotonous practice. Such an emotional charge would result from the mundane world but would be singled out from it and/or would single out from it. We all know this type of enhancement. That is why a boring Sunday walk differs from an inspiring one, a neutral from a love-enriched life-world, a dull day of work from a fulfilling one, a dead sunrise from a sparkling one and so forth. The examples you mention within the framework of your "story of happiness" are mainly very good ones for such an intrinsic enhancement out of everyday life, which nevertheless leaves everyday life only far behind.

---

4   https://www.zeit.de/wissen/2014-03/bier-hefe-erbgut-biologie-syntetisch

Intrinsic enhancement – out of everyday life

For years and sometimes two, three, four times a week I used to 'celebrate' watching the sunset (as an almost daily 'rite') at the edge of the Aubinger Lohe (woodlands on a hill at the western edge of Munich) behind my parents' house in my younger days. Watching these sunsets became a habit. At the same time, because sunsets embrace a certain enhancement – without any influence, interpretation or projection on it from the outside – they were not daily routine, after all. But they were a breakthrough of daily routine that was marked by (school) constraints, daily duties, heartless and senseless realities of adult life (car, money, prestige, avarice, fights in a relationship, power politics, small talk, TV ...) They were something out of the ordinary; and the sunsets had nothing of an exaltation, they were neither emotionally numbing nor deadening: They allowed at any time the quiet sounds or even highlighted them – the so-called 'small nature' (in the meaning of Adalbert Stifter).

And from this intrinsic enhancement out of everyday life (and beyond it) a boundary experience can arise. The transitions however seem to be smooth here. At least something similar occurred to me occasionally. And then the sunsets gained a momentum of boundary experience; at least a strong ecstatic element that drew me out of myself and dragged me in this promising light. Mostly a 'strong' mental experience remained. It seldom increased to a mental boundary experience. But once it became a physical experience taking it to the limit: I once happened to celebrate the sunset during a storm at the seaside in Corsica, I ventured myself on and on the promontory being somehow drawn and lured there. At last I wanted to sit and contemplate at the very front facing the raging sea and waves 'making up' a poem. And then a huge wave came rolling along, unlike all the other waves I had been closely watching during the last hour, since it was clear to me that I was in mortal danger. This monster wave surprised and flooded me. I made every effort to cling to the rocks. This huge wave would have washed me into the swirling and roaring sea where I would have been smashed and crushed into pieces on the sharp-edged rocks.

Big wave of San Vito

What I want to say is: The transitions are smooth and simultaneously, depending on the intensity, there is a leap of experience which leaves everyday life behind. I am not of the opinion that this type of boundary experience (necessarily) deadens the sense of heart. It is the exact opposite: When threatened by death, ecstasy, frenzy, madness, etc. we gain awareness where in our world the true values and qualities are and where not. Your own heart only knows after such an experience where it really clung and clings to and how much certain people, animals, plants, landscapes, places etc. meant and mean to your heart.

Stifter, Landauer and Alexis Zorba

Let me quote (pp. 28–30) some of the numerous subtle and profound passages from your presentation: "Why do we like to flee and devalue everyday life and daily activities? In the Biedermeier period [...] small things were in great demand for a short period of time. Adalbert Stifter wrote in 1853: 'So when we are talking about 'great' and 'small' things now, let me present my views, which will certainly differ from those of many other people. What I consider great is the breeze of the wind, the ripple of water, the growth of crops, the undulation of the sea, the greening of the earth, the shininess of the sky, the shimmer of stars: The gorgeously approaching thunderstorm, the lightning that splits houses, the storm driving the surf, the fire-spitting mountain, the earthquake burying landscapes I do not consider greater than the previous phenomena ...'[5] Stifter found many admirers, some among them that one would not expect right away, e.g. the German anarchist Gustav Landauer – who was murdered in 1919. In a letter to his friend he wrote about a book in 1903: 'The avoidance of all gross effects the calm choppiness of the whole thing is beautiful and reminding me of our greatest master, Stifter[6]. It is the graceful softness and serenity' in 'connection with the visual perception of nature' (p. 138) by which Landauer is attracted and solely through which the success of a revolution can be justified in his opinion. This revolution has not happened yet until now. Nature seems to fade away. We have forgotten to be appealed by these phenomena to a sufficient extent. We concentrate instead on forces that 'lie behind' or on extraordinary events and on 'gross effects.''

Lake Plöckenstein. Stifter visited, celebrated and described this lonely lake in his homeland

5   Adalbert Stifter: Bunte Steine, Pest 1853, preface
6   Hanna Delf von Wolzogen in: Geborgenheit und Gefährdung in der epischen und
     malerischen Welt Adalbert Stifters, ed. by J. Enklaar et al., Würzburg 2006, p. 133

You are making use of Stifter and his way of experiencing and describing nature – and also the terrific clue about Landauer's reception of it and its embedding into revolutionary thoughts (which certainly is something out of the ordinary). However, we should not forget that Stifter was not only quite a melancholy and romantic character, but also a strongly phlegmatic one – which distinguishes him from the romanticists. He just looks for those atmospheric aspects of nature that correspond to his temper. Stifter may convey the small moments, but as they are not common, they give some special charm to his stories. And at the same time it shows quite beautifully how each character seeks out and celebrates the scenery and nature experience that is so close to his soul.

Stifter lived in a post-Romantic period, and the society had no longer interest in animism, but all the more in the Biedermeier experience of nature and parks on Sundays. At the latest, however, when writing about his grandparents, something from an older period is to be heard, something older to which also the romanticists referred, and something that may have survived in the rural society: the quasi late animistic world of (local) legends. (Cf. the following lengthy Stifter quotation: "At that time I often thought how such an unspeakable swarm of unearthly things and outrageous experiences in the life of a single person, of my great grandfather, could have existed and how ordinary and exposed everything is now – no spirit can be seen or heard, and when father is held back at night, it is bad forest ways or an unexpected rainfall. Oh yes, my grandmother used to say, when things like that came up for discussion, 'everything is decreasing, the bird in the air and the fish in the water. When formerly at the twelfthtide or Saturday night some weeping or calling was clearly to be heard from the Pfingstgraben [a local moat] or the Hammerau [a local place close to the river], so today everything is quiet and dead in these areas now, seldom can we encounter a ghost light (ignis fatuus) or a merman sitting at the river bank. Today people do no longer have such a strong belief as they used to have in earlier days, although the elder ones who told these stories were no fools either, but were fearless, enlightened men. The youth readily wants to know everything better, but as time goes by, it reconciles with the talking of the elder ones and admits to do so.' This is what my grandmother used to say; but I listened to her with eagerly watching eyes and did not have to hit on her words; because I strongly loved to believe everything."[7] ...

---

7   Adalbert Stifter: Die Mappe meines Urgroßvaters (1841), in: Studien, vol 2, ed. by B. Adler, Berlin 1923, pp. 5–209, here: pp. 12–13

Another example with somewhat different experiences of nature and the sense of heart openings could be presented with the fictional character of Alexis Zorba (whose author – Nikos Kazantzakis – is inspired by the life-philosophical tradition). I did so once in an essay. Zorba is like Stifter very empathetic and compassionate, at the same time southern and sanguine. He is strongly prone to ecstatically bursting or existentially precipitous experiences and exaltations. But always with a very strong sense of heart and always solidary with the oppressed, the outsiders, and marginalized people. He is an anarchist as well as Landauer, but more casual, rooted to the soil, heartier ...

Ways to opening the sense of heart

Now how can we achieve the opening, strengthening and sensitisation of the sense of heart? I think, there are several ways and means. Sometimes the breaking-up and bursting open of mundane or civilizing or technical routines may be crucial and sometimes the calm and quiet acceptance of the small occurrences/gestures/things/creatures of nature and the human world. What is important after all is a certain quality of your heart: so that your heart can (cor)respond and argue once warmly once in a heated way. I once pursued these responses in an essay about the phenomenon of heartwarming places. We know such places from our childhood already. Those places are often linked with intensive experiences: The hidden spot in the forest where we built a tree house or played with fire; the near-derelict cellar in a ruined building tagged 'Do not enter!' etc. Even the heartwarming places we cherish as adults often disclose themselves in their conciseness and significance only until they are threatened (by demolition or control structures). So here again: in a boundary threat the heart recognizes what it truly clings to and becomes fully aware of it (often afterwards only.)

Perhaps we could say that the following aspects are important or necessary for the opening and sensitisation of the sense of heart: everyday world experiences, work experience, work as such in one's life-world. Of equal importance are laughing and weeping a lot – together with the boundary experiences that may look out from behind. But also even more fundamental than anything else is that you could get from your mum, from society, from the world in general, a good deal of basic trust and also experience from all the last-mentioned. Well, to put it in a nutshell: to trust your own heart as well as the 'heart of the world'...

What do you think?

Cordially yours

R. J. K.

3

Authentic Nature Experience and Distance Towards Nature

Rudolf Gaßenhuber   March 22, 2016

Dear Mr Kozljanič,

I find your letter very agreeable and interesting, particularly your endeavour to differentiate between the inner and exterior enhancement resp. emotional charge. What does real experience mean, what is artificial and hysterical we could ask. What is life, what is decadence? This is our main topic, I think. Is this correct? Before dealing with it let me shortly examine our three further possible differences, which I rather consider not really to be differences.

A) *Assessment of boundary experiences*

You mention intensively experienced sunsets right up to a real threat of a monster wave, and you write: "I do not think that this type of boundary experience (must) deaden(s) the sense of heart." Well, I don't think so either. As stated above, "a disease, blows of fate, and other critical boundary experiences" can reopen the sense of heart. Well, a "storm" often is the case. We have more or less concurring views her, I think. We only take different starting points. You start with the example of the "simply mundane, banal, love-neutral, obtuse, salvaging-salvaged routine and also boring, grey and monotonous practice." You start with the colour grey asking yourself how this grey can become colourful again. I start my deliberations with positive examples of the mundane, the colourful, the sky amidst lush greenery asking myself where the stars might have disappeared. This different starting point may transport a different assessment: When starting off with this grey, the colourful can hardly be vivid enough. When starting from the colourful you are careful when facing shrill colours.

Your idea of comparing Zorba and Stifter is delightful and profound. We see in both of them similar starting points. On the one hand there is the clumsy, young, and rich Englishman who is taken into a school of life by a strongman. In the end the guy is pecuniary poorer it is true, but richer in fullness of life. On the other hand there is the spiritual profusion of Stifter – thank you for this passage: "... such an unspeakable swarm of unearthly things and outrageous experiences" marking the life of his grandfather. Stifter's main concern is to conserve or to save some of this abundance (of life).

Zorba's topic is augmentation, the liberation of life's stimuli, bursting the chains of rational, calculating life and the opening for an instant fullness of life and dance. With Stifter, however, there is no need for augmentation, he rather has to protect himself from overstimulation. He is the one who still believes his grandmother, he is the guardian of her world.

B) *Power and dominance*

The topic of distance towards nature should be approached with the criticism of power, civilization, and capitalism. You are absolutely right here. Everything is involved here, of course. But what I meant is the distance towards nature is the deep beginning, which is not seen by Marx and subsequent left-wingers in their affinity for technology that can hardly be shattered. The idea of the dominance over nature is a widespread ideal among left-wingers – and not only there. Due to this theory the solution lies in the relations of production and not in the productive forces. Marx himself was deeply enthusiastic by technical advance. The downside of this development was not noted at that time. The better phrase in question would read. "Initially a good deal of the problems humanity has is not of politico-economic origin but from our own tremendous distance towards nature." It is only in the course of growing empowerment when the naked object is invented, which is deprived of all that is soulful and soullike: This technical side of the distance towards nature probably equals power and empowerment. The mental side of it is a retreat of the soul into its inner sphere. The forced loss of soulful places is a reason and a consequence of civilization, capitalization, acceleration, and globalization. Formerly meaningful, vital necessities end up in a museum at best.

C) *Shamanism*

Shamans – main mediators or emergency helpers? The "visionary (mythical and animistic) access to nature": Was it an access for everybody or was a shaman needed? In your last letter you leave out the word shaman and speak of "visionary (mythical and animistic)" and previously of "shamanistic-visionary". Shamans were specialists of trance and the mediation with Gods. I think that people then did not need any specialists for their main access to their ancestors, to the landscape, to the animals. The main access took place in daily contact with all beings dwelling around them. Only in cases of emergency was a shaman involved. Your image of it varies here: Free versus regulated visionary experiences. I would say in short: Nature religion versus transcendent religion. Certainly, all this may be answered empirically, and we can defer it for the moment.

D) *Perception*

Now I will move on to the question that interests and occupies me the most: What is perception, what is experiencing? This is the reason why I read your book "Freundschaft mit der Natur" ("Friendship with Nature"). The longer I deal with it, the better I like it. It is an important opening out from a two-valued phenomenology towards the richness of real, multi-valued experience. The two-valued logic of phenomenology likes to describe only two accesses at a time – dead or alive, coin or trash and such. In the standard example of Husserl's dummy we first experience a dummy (a dummy sits in a display window) and then a living woman (the shop had engaged an actress). Heidegger sees the forest as a supplier of wood or as a living being. For critics of reductionism a tear is either saltwater or perceptible grief. In Gestalt Psychology the images switch between the old and young woman, vase or couple. To my mind these are simplifications, reprehensible simplifications and one-sidedness. Here your book is a beneficial opening whilst bringing various occidental accesses to nature together with approaches to natural philosophy. Besides we all know how important our attitudes are towards the counterpart for the counterpart's experiencing: Is the woman in the display window a stranger, a neighbour or our lover? Our experiencing changes radically through an emotional bond! Is the difference between stranger and lover less important than that between dummy and actress? Here the crucial question arises: Which examples do we choose? Which example affects our life, is really the formal switch from death to life? No, I think the example is rather constructed and extremely rare in real life. The switch from stranger to confidant (friend and foe and nuances) is much more obvious. We walk through the city and often ask ourselves, do I know him, must I, may I greet him? Oscillating like this is fundamental for our daily life and is even practiced by one-year-olds.

Rofan mountains

I think, I can tell you more exactly now what pleased me about your dormouse story and why it is so touching when you thank the Rofan mountains[1]. Not only a friendship with 'nature' is speaking here, but a specific connection to a 'this one'. Well, this distinction is the key to the very shibboleth between affinity and distance towards nature. The aborigines live together with their landmarks, i.e. ancestors, i.e. biographic and mythological tales. Geography, biography, historiography, and mythology tell the same significant tale. For the ancient Greeks as well the old Gods had specific places, the Olympus was this mountain and the Nymph of the Spring was, at least initially, this specific

---

1   Robert Josef Kozljanič: Freundschaft mit der Natur – Naturphilosophische Praxis
     und Tiefenökologie, Klein Jasedow 2008, p. 9.

spring. You certainly could tell of this much more than I do. The "genius loci" is not only an equivalent of the atmosphere of a place, but also of our intimacy, remembrance, heart-opening and emotional bond. I would like to talk more about it with you. Where do I find your essay about the heart-warming places? A phenomenology of sheer atmospheres without the topic of the inner emotional bond and involvement would only mean new reductionism.

At last I like to outline a rough and provisional scheme of perception, which may facilitate our further conversation. Please note this photograph.

Álfastein, an inviting group of rocks in Kópavogur, Iceland

It is a group of rocks in Iceland, where fairies are said to dwell according to local knowledge. In order not to disturb the fairies the new built street – as we can see – was conducted around the rocks.

The rocks were neither removed nor displaced.

Now, please imagine – many years ago – you came upon a similar arrangement of rocks in an uninhabited area. The following might happen to you:

1. *First impression, pleasure:*

You perceive the group, you like it, perhaps the nice and warm sun is shining on it, it invites you to sit, to lay down, to linger. You lie there chatting and resting.

2. *Recognition, joy of reunion:*

After a few days you may go there again. You recognize the rocks. You are glad. The earlier experience strengthens a first feeling of familiarity.

3. *Further recognition, habit:*

Your recognition becomes a habit. Step by step the rock forms a solid place in your ramble. It is a good place for a rest, a chat with others and simply being there. A good spirit dwells here, there is a good mood. You make friends with this place, it grows dear to your heart, it grows on you. This would be a strong reason not to spoil forever this nature idyll with buildings.

4. *Negativity:*

You can come here even in bad weather if a storm surprises you. Not only the good spirits are present here. It can be murky and uncanny.

5. *Specification of spirits:*

Imaginative people from your group turn the well-perceived atmosphere into lovely stories with helpful fairies. The positive about the stories and the positive of this place are still so close together, albeit a symbolization and a first gaining of independence is taking place. The telling of these stories and invocating the spirits also helps to stabilize the good atmosphere and to banish worse feelings for instance.

6. *Generations:*

Imagine, you have been living in this area for a long time. Points 1-5 are stories your grandparents told you from your ancestors when they came into this land. The ancestors were buried or burnt to ashes not far from the group of rocks. Their memories passed into the rocks. You associate these memories with many rests at this place and establish a connection with your ancestors. The whole world is made of beings of the most different kind and each action is social action.

7. *Regional gods and myths:*

Their worldview does not only comprise local Gods like the fairies, but also encompassing cosmic deities like Father Heaven, Mother Earth, and the Lord of Animals. Great tales are told how everything began and the fairies are entangled into this myth, too. The myths are still closely connected with phenomena, they entangle human experiencing with natural phenomena to produce a united cosmic reality.

8. *Idealization and centralization:*

With sedentariness, agriculture, and animal husbandry the population rapidly grows. Hierarchic, specialized societies emerge. Regional religions are co-opted, integrated or become extinct. An enormous process of standardization and centralization sets in. In the philosophical field Plato contrives the first attempt of an idealistic system where the real world appears a shadow of the ideal world. The real phenomenon itself is deducted from reality. Finally from these beginnings the conception of object arises, which is defined by primary, measurable qualities. The real, the subject of science departs from the perceived phenomena. The secondary qualities are deferred to the subjected and private. The qualities of bonding and relationships in western thinking (unlike in the East) under point 1-3 are no longer added on to the relevant qualities of things. Now we are talking about the attribute-substance relation and view the substances as the true, hard reality.

9. *Science and technology:*

The programme of increasing knowledge, wealth and power is gaining momentum. The first experimental science (Roger Bacon) is still linked directly to the power of the church (Clemens IV). The aim of understanding the world anew is the increase of power (not theoria), and science is a means. Columbus, Francis Bacon and others follow. Two completely different views on our rocks arise. From a mineralogical perspective, it is decomposed into its constituents, identified in its minerals, clarified in its chemical structure. Its development in earth's history is unravelled from a geological and glaciological point of view and its transport during the last ice age until its present place.

10. *Poetic existence:*

In music and poetry nature is extolled or serves as a trigger for a poet's panoply of thoughts. This is a picture of a relatively big rock, which supplies for Nietzsche the material equivalent of the philosopher's deepest and most serious ideas: the eternal resurgence.

The so-called Nietzsche Stone at Lake Silvaplana in the Upper Engadine, Switzerland

"I stopped at a massive, pyramidal and towering block of stone not far from Surlei. Then I had this idea." For Nietzsche the idea of eternal resurgence was the "highest formula of affirmation". For him the stone represents its unalterable, dire past, the 'It was'. Ire/inward wrath, discontent and revenge change into a 'but this is what I wanted!' – the stone as a symbol and materialization of his unalterable, unredeemable, merciless past. The stone acts as a trigger of an idea that removes itself far away from the stone.

Where does the deadening of feelings begin, soul-loss, the pre-stage of destructiveness? You write: "artificial (metaphysical/ideological) ... the exalted, the deadening". Yes, but what is the artificial, the man-made that eliminates us from the phenomenon and deepens the loss of the world through circularity? Where exactly does the "emotional charge" begin? This is an exciting question. Is it already the magical interpretations, the trolls and fairies that transform the magic of the place into a magic of imagination? Are fairy tales already artificial or merely rewarding, animating or eliminative? Is it the religions, the concept of monotheism or only materialism that disenchants the world? Or is man himself a distanced creature that takes a stand and has always installed a world of his own around and inside nature? Where does the pathological, the decadent character begin?

In my opinion the problems start at point 5 already. Authentic feelings, affections and bonds in their first derivative of a spiritual realm are cast here. The consequence is a de-regionalization and centralization, philosophy and monotheism, science and technology. Regional bonds like 'my beloved rock' lose their importance and rights and titles of ownership superpose the emotional bonding. The meaning of a beloved person recedes in favour of possession. The Álfastone in Iceland is an absolute curiosity. By tendency, atmospheres, memories, and emotional bonds are disdained or neglected in general.

The 'heart' shrinks constantly and matters less and less. The nice solution – as you write – would be "confidence into your own heart as well as into the 'heart of the world'". How can this be achieved? I know psychological answers only. This is what I often experienced. But as far as society and politics are concerned I feel overwhelmed, and with regard to humanity as a whole, I am rather pessimistic.

Kind regards

R. G.

Robert J. Kozljanič   May 9, 2016

Dear Mr Gaßenhuber

At the moment there is too much going on at all levels (work, philosophy, family, friends ...). I can hardly figure out how to free myself from the exuberant everyday life and not so ordinary tasks and obligations (both occurring quite mixed at the moment); at the same time I am trying to be a connoisseur of the art of living by not losing completely out of sight my own passions and pleasures of life; or as Romans would express it: to assign to one's genius what it deserves and not to frustrate and to weaken it by ambition and avarice, performance and functioning and other types of modern and post-modern superego dominances.

At the same time, I don't want to wait too long answering you, hence a little compromise. I am sending you the part I have already written, the first part so to speak, but I haven't had the time to deal with the question you are most interested in, as you wrote in your last email: Where does authentic nature experience and the description of nature turn into ideologization, decadent emotional charge, and distance or alienation from nature. Or in your words: "Where does the deadening of feelings begin, the soul-loss, the pre-stage of destructiveness?" I hope to find the time to answer respectively to respond soon. For me too, this question is pivotal. For today, however, here are some remarks, footnotes, and possible preliminary considerations concerning the first half of your email.

I can readily accept the summary of our three great subjects – evaluation of "boundary experiences", "power and dominance", "shamanism". If I comment here, then I am far from meaning to correct you – because there is nothing to be corrected – but I do so in terms of an amplification and reassurance.

Ad *A) "Assessment of boundary experiences"*

From the grey and drab we are longing for the colourful, which often enough – when getting too grey or really awful (for in my case too much grey means almost horrible) – turns out to be shrill. Viewed from the (Apollonian) colourful angle, standing in the (Apollonian) colourful world the problem of the grey colour (of Hades) is not so urgent. At the same time we are sceptical towards loud and shrill exaltations, as you describe so splendidly. For they could be hysterical overreactions of a decadent (hyper-civilized) spirit alienated from nature. But they could also be the Dionysic clearance kick, which – quite comprehensibly – comes off the stronger the longer it was horribly oppressed or sedated beforehand. One has to check carefully in each individual case.

How lovely you symbolically outlined the point around which our ideas revolve. What you show and what is shown here: Everything depends on the context and the point of view and what goal/ideal we have in mind, too. And all the different relations and tendencies arise from this point. In this sense these are relative conditions albeit certainly not arbitrary ones. If we want to approach these contexts, a substance/object/notion ontology is not much of a help, what we need are, so to speak, hermeneutics of context and differential diagnosis. As far as I can see we agree in this basic tendency.

Ad *B) "Power and dominance"*

What you write about Marx, for instance, and the left-wingers that followed him, about their (partly blind) enthusiasm for technology, progress and also the dominance of nature hits a central point. And then I ask myself, how shall I deal with it – as a person whose heart beats on the left? I have tried to develop a leftist position[2] that is not marked by distance towards nature, but closeness and love for nature, a position that does not play off man against nature, whose solidarity does not cover humans only (or even: only a class of humans – workers) but shows solidarity with all those who are oppressed, enslaved, exploited, and/or destroyed by power and dominance – it is also solidary with places, landscapes, plants, animals, indigenous peoples, according to the motto: "Exploited of all countries show solidarity!" And I could show by reprinting two texts by Theodor Lessing that there is a different left-wing tradition, as I hope: A tradition of solidary democracy of life. It was only yesterday that I discovered an interesting passage in a book by Michel Onfray[3] where Onfray differentiates between a Dionysic and an embittered left. "The Dionysic left says radically 'yes'

---

2   In: Theodor Lessing / Robert Josef Kozljanič: Untergang der Erde am Geist der Machteliten. Die verfluchte Kultur der Maschine. 100 Jahre Zivilisationskritik und solidarische Lebensdemokratie, München 2014

3   Michel Onfray: Im Namen der Freiheit. Leben und Philosophie des Albert Camus, München 2015

[... and] turns its back on the embittered left, which says 'no'. The former feeds on the life instinct, the latter on the death instinct." (p. 164)

The embittered "socialism was based on the sick thinking of revolutionaries who sought less the joyful positive power than the negative satisfaction of destroying everything that hindered their seizure of power". (p. 165) Well, Onfray paints this contrast far too rigid, radical, bold and simple – quite shrill as you would put it. In view of his own history of oppression he may be pardoned. Another question arises whether Onfray's notion of freedom based on his radically individualistic and hedonistically materialistic view can be the right one – as it always stands for the freedom from (doing) something instead of the freedom for (doing) something – so, can he adequately represent and/or explicate the other tradition, which is a nature- and life-friendly one? His hints, however, are real and important. And what Onfray writes about Camus as the representative of this Dionysic left and Camus' fidelity to his origins and the related down-to-earthness with it, and what he tells about his closeness to life and people catches our attention. "Camus was not a man of resentment, but a man of loyalty. No reader of the 'First Man', however patient, will find a passage where he demonises the powerful whom he held responsible for the poverty of his family. There was no hatred in him for the French state that sent his father to the front and to his death. He did not say a bad word about the employers of his mother, who worked as a domestic servant. [...] Bitter socialism is dark and thanatophilic. Dionysian socialism is entirely devoted to fidelity. Camus never forgot where he came from." (p. 166–167) "With Camus, as with Nietzsche, the critique of embittered socialism is not a critique of socialism, but of embitterment [...]. Their rejection of despotic socialism is a rejection of despotism, not of socialism. For socialism can feed on other sources; it does not need the black waters of bitterness. Affirmative loyalty, Dionysian concern and life under the sun can serve as its basis. Camus loved life, he wanted life and wished to make it richer in possibilities for himself and others." (p. 167–168) When taking a closer look, we can find a similar fidelity to ancestry and to the native land/landscape/locality with Onfray. His life and actions show it. Nonetheless as far as my limited knowledge about Onfray permits a judgement, I do not see this point (yet) adequately apprehended/reviewed in his own philosophical deliberations.

Ad *C)* *"Shamanism"*

Here again you come up with a crucial point, a rather blurred than clarified one in my deliberations so far. And here again I would like to express my sincere thanks: Thank you for these eye-opening thoughts. The principal question is: Does the mythical and animistic access to nature need a shamanistic specialist, a kind of proto-priest? An expert on visions who conveys/deduces/interprets the access to the daimonic-divine nature? You say no: "I think that people then did not need any specialists for their main access to their ancestors, to the landscape, to the animals. The main access took place in daily contact with all beings dwelling around them. Only in cases of emergency was a shaman involved". And I can only agree with you with all my heart! So why do I always invoke the shaman in order to illustrate the mythical, animistic, visionary access towards nature? It is because he represents this access in its extreme form on the one hand – thus showing it concisely. On the other hand the archaic shamanism shows to my mind that there was and is an intrinsically natural and sensory 'religion', a 'religion' which, to my mind, does not need to leave behind and diabolise the body, the senses, and the sensory world and to flee into a 'pure' hereafter – a radical transcendence.

A third reason is that shamanism is quite an open and flexible system, which still works with a cosmic, natural basic structure, makes even sense today, and is appealing for the lover of nature: The three perceptible sensory main levels of the world (netherworld, earth, sky) and the four cardinal directions. Maybe I secretly proceed too strongly from a shamanistic image that is shaped by my 'favourite shaman' Tahca Ushte – and also by the experiences I personally had with the Lakota shaman Elmer Norbert Running. Do you know the book about Tahca Ushte, resp. his English name, John Fire Lame Deer? The title is: "Tahca Ushte. Seeker of Visions. The Life of a Sioux Medicine Man", co-authored with the artist Richard Erdoes. I can highly recommend it to you. Tahca Ushte is the Amerindian version of Alexis Zorba, the book is not only most interesting, it is also full of vital energy, humaneness, worldly wisdom and humour. – But nevertheless: Your reservation towards shamanism remains. What I am willing to overlook and neglect, perhaps because of a somewhat too romantic image of the shaman: With shamanism some sort of first priesthood, priestly ideology, and clergy arises, sometimes so rudimentary that it can be neglected; but sometimes uncompromising and tough, especially (and according to Ruth Benedict's book "Patterns of Culture") in the so-called Apollonian cultures (often cultures of planters and cultivators). A good (tough) example are the Kogi or Kagaba shamans in the north of Colombia in the Caribbean coastal mountain range of the Sierra Nevada de Santa Marta; and another not quite so severe example are the Hopi. The situation is a bit different with the Lakota, who are "Dionysic" cultures (mostly hunters and gatherers) according to Benedict. Here the shamans are not organized in priestly casts. Here more individualism and more individual experience seem possible and are even required and encouraged. A completely dogmatically regulated religion and morality administrated by priests is not to be found there. In his vocational vision Elmer Norbert Running for instance had the mission to help all people of all skin colour. When the shamans of his people in the mid/end 90s decided to end the time of openness (since the 70s) due to the bad experiences they had had with the exploitation of their religion by the white man, Elmer was almost the only one who allowed Caucasians to attend the sun dance. His tribesmen accepted it. But as the view at the whole phenomenon of shamanism shows, there are by no means only such relatively open and individual shamans. Where the visionary force wanes and the experience with these religious sources no longer lavishly flows and cultures (have to) lead a stricter and specialized life the dogmatic and priestly moments come to the fore. I understand all too well that you are sceptical as far as the beginning of ideological and emotional charge, superstructure and oppression are concerned. I am sceptical here, too. In my concept of shamanism it hardly happens that shamans are often viewed as outsiders within their own communities. One is afraid of them, but, occasionally, they are needed in serious cases if people do not know what to do. Well, at bottom, our way of dealing with our physicians is not much different. It is almost something like love-hate. And it is not only motivated by philistine feelings (but arguably always subliminally in danger of being co-motivated in a philistine way! For in any society, outsiders have a tough job with ordinary people however positive they may be); but also due to the fact that shamans are really odd guys. Sometimes it is difficult to see where the line is between healing magic and harmful magic – but also between truth and manipulation, between help and self-interest. I once had the honour of making the acquaintance of two Nepalese village shamans and watching them shamanize. Later they told me: At every initiation into shamanism, together with a good shaman, a harmful sorcerer/witch is brought into being, thereby the connection is compulsory! I.e. white and black magic are inseparably linked with each other.

This is all for today. I hope to be able to send you the second part soon.

Kind regards

R. J. K.

Robert J. Kozljanič　　　　　　　　　　　　　　　　June 2, 2016

Dear Mr Gaßenhuber

well, as promised, here is the second part of my answer. Let me address your key question: When does authentic nature experience and description of nature turn into ideologisation, a decadent charge of feelings, and distance towards nature resp. alienation towards nature? Or in your words: "Where does the deadening of feelings begin, soul-loss, the pre-stage of destructiveness?"

You try to determine the intrinsic point in question by means of an outline (which I subsequently partly enlarged and partly formulated with my own words) encompassing 10 steps of a process of determining a local experience or, more generally, a process of becoming a reality:

1. First pleasant, aesthetic experiencing and getting to know a place, a group of rocks (e.g. Àlfastein prior to any type of construction).

2. Confidence-inspiring recognition resp. reunion with the rocks: the meeting is deepened and becomes a ful experience.

3. Further (establishment of a relationship due to) recognition resp. experiencing in the sense of growing fond of the group of rocks, which thereby becomes a heart-warming place, a place of habit(ation).

4. First negative experiences making the (accidental or essential) drawbacks of the group of rocks come to light. – You mention the example of a thunderstorm. This could be integrated without any problems into the aesthetic experiencing; the aesthetic of the sublime, the overwhelming and threatening, of course, no longer the aesthetic of the beautiful and the idyllic. Nonetheless: Until now the experience of the place would still remain within the framework of my so-called modern-aesthetic access to nature.

5. Due to metaphorizing and symbolizing activities of imagination the aesthetic place becomes a place of spirits. This leads to a certain assumption of an independent reality/specification of spirits (and the spiritual) in tales and first rites. – Here one could add, if I am right, the symbolic-allegoric access to nature – but with the emphasis on the symbolic. (As for the emphasis on the allegoric see under point 8.) But how shall we deal with the archaic-mythical-daimonic access to nature insofar as it is, in my

opinion, a daimonic-visionary one, too? Shall we introduce it here or not – whilst you are talking initially about imaginary fancies and imagination-symbolizations? We have not talked about visions so far.

6. An oral tradition of tales overlapping generations evolves and to the previous cult of place joins an ancestor cult. The stories that are told about the group of rocks thereby become aesthetic, fanciful-daimonic and fantastic ones with reference to the ancestor cult. – You write: "The whole world consist of beings of all kind, all types of action is social action".

7. Near-natural and trans-regional cosmologies/mythologies evolve: Encompassing divinities like Father Sky, Mother Earth, Lord/Lady of the animals appear. – And with all that probably, what I call the "Olympic, mythical, atmospheric access to nature". So here something could happen (what we can observe with Greek sanctuaries: cf. my "The Spirit of a Place"-monograph vol. 1, point 3.2 and 3.3.[4]) that our embosomed and meanwhile tradition-rich group of rocks is reshaped by an Olympic divinity:

The group of rocks and the demons clinging to it are, so to speak, in an Apollonian sanctuary now: reshaped but not overbuilt by Apollo.

Apollon temple Delphi

---

4   Robert Josef Kozljanič: Der Geist eines Ortes. Kulturgeschichte und Phänomenologie des Genius Loci, 2 vols. München 2004.

8. Now the transformation of the Axial Age occurs, in our case: the platonic ideo-logization with its tendency to standardization, idealization, hierarchization, centralization and objectification: Thereby the nature-near and heart-near metaphorization and symbolization of the group of rocks would shift to a strong emphasis on transcending allegorisation and abstraction. – This would be a symbolically-allegoric access to nature – or in better terms: a symbolically-allegoric overcoming of nature, but precisely with an emphasis on the (rationally-)allegoric one. – Linked with this life-afterlife split is a first matter-form, a body-spirit, and an object-subject split. All heart-warming, sensually-presenting, relation-causing qualities of our group of rocks have either vanished into the hereafter and/or are relocated into the subject now (or as deducted and deficient epiphenomena by the grace of the hereafter tolerated in situ). Therefore they are either transcendent or just subjectively perceived.

9. Global dominance, technologization, scientification of nature, instrumentalization: The modern science oriented access to nature has started its triumph. As you write: "Two completely different views on our rocks arise. From a mineralogical perspective, it is decomposed into its constituents, identified in its minerals, clarified in its chemical structure. Its development in earth's history is unravelled from a geological and glaciological point of view and its transport during the last Ice Age until its present place." The rocks are reduced to a scientific object. At least for the positivistic 'hardliner', they are now deprived of all emotional, aesthetic, mythical, religious properties: dead.

10. Modern art, one could say, finally conveys an ultimately aestheticistic revival of place. By revolving around himself, the modern artist elicits from the object the qualities, characteristics, associations of impression subjectivised in point 8 and plays his individualistic game with them. You write so pointedly that nature serves "as a trigger for a poet's panoply of thoughts". "The stone acts as a trigger of an idea that removes itself far away from the stone." (E.g. the Nietzsche Stone not far from Surlei).

The Question of the turning point: nature – alienation I

So where is the turning point we are looking for? The point where authentic, personal, heart-warming and dialogic experience of nature starts to become an alienated, overly intellectual, exploiting and a heart-hardened use and straightening of nature? You write: "In my opinion the problems start at point 5 already. Authentic feelings, affections and bonds in their first derivative of a spiritual realm are cast here. The consequence is a de-regionalization and centralization, philosophy and monotheism, science and technology. Regional bonds like 'my beloved rock' lose their importance and rights and titles of ownership superpose the emotional bonding. The meaning of a beloved person recedes to the benefit of possession."

A priori I agree within the scope of your characterization (which contains an enormous clarifying and differentiating potential). The only problem I can see is that your characterization/development/interpretation moves at one position (in the sense of a change into a different class of explanation, of a *metábasis eis állo génos*). And this is exactly between point 4 and 5. Up to point 4, you are assuming the experience of a modern (or postmodern) person today: A human profane and enlightened by tendency, but at the same time a lover of nature, emotionally open with certain aesthetically-contemplative basic tendencies. Therefore everything you write up to point 4 is pretty easy to understand and to affirm from such a human's perspective. Under point 5 spirits are coming into play now. Now it is getting problematic in several aspects. On the one hand, because ghosts do not belong to the (officially accepted) contemporary Western way of life. Secondly, because the previous sensual-aesthetic level of the bodily sensed external world is abruptly abandoned. The imagination and its fantasies and projections come to the fore. The external world is completely transformed and superstructured by the internal world. At the same time the well-known assessments lurk in the background: Tangible in the outer world = real, tangible in the inner world = tendentially unreal. Thirdly because now you are choosing another methodical access, as I see it. Until now your argumentation was synchronous from the point of view of a present nature lover. But now you start to reason diachronically and historically, for with points 5-10 we enter a historical reflection and interpretation of occidental site-experience processes – from animistic beginnings over polytheism, monotheism to positivism and aestheticism. The third reason in particular leads me to speaking about a leap, a *metábasis*.

Interagentivity: socio-natural interrelations

In order to avoid this leap a diachronic and historical approach is mandatory from the beginning.

One should start from the earliest animistic Álfastéin experiences resp. from the analogue rock experiences among archaic hunter-gatherer cultures. The present point 5 would become the new point 1 then and amalgamate with point 6, but in a way that a fantastic-projective imagination cannot be assumed at this level, but only an environmental and interactive empirical and semantic level, which would be located prior to a thislife-afterlife division, previous to all matter-form, body-spirit and object-subject division. If I am right, one would be pretty much at the level described by Tim Ingold (whom I have read in the meantime, owing to your hint): "In the hunter-gatherer economy of knowledge [of course, instead of speaking of an "economy of knowledge", I would rather speak of a "way of life and worldly wisdom"], by contrast, it is as entire persons, not as disembodied minds, that human beings engage with one another and, moreover, with non-human beings as well. They do so as beings *in* a world, not as minds which, excluded from a given reality, find themselves in the common predicament of having to make sense of it. To coin a term, the constitutive quality of their world is not intersubjectivity but *interagentivity*. To speak of the forest as a parent is not, then, to model object relations in terms of primary intersubjectivity, but to recognize that at root, the constitutive quality of intimate relations with non-humans and human components of the environment is one and the same"[5].

Precisely because there is no separation within the scope of this intimate and intensive man-nature relationship, interagentivity also means that we do not make a strict separation neither between human and non-human imagination nor between human and non-human spirits (in the sense of daimons). (Under the keyword "perception" you were aiming at something quite similar when speaking about "oscillating"; a nice term for it.) Ingold demonstrates it quite well in his example about the Aboriginal experience and interpretation of landscape: their 'dreamtime landscape' with 'dreamtime paths' and 'dreamtime places'. "Places, however, can possess meaning at different levels. Some have a fundamental spiritual potency connected with the Distant Time story of their creation. Some, were people have died, are avoided for as long as memory persists. Others, again, are known for particular hunting events or other personal experiences of encounters with animals. On all of these levels – spiritual, historical, personal – the landscape

---

5   Tim Ingold: Hunting and Gathering as Ways of Perceiving the Environment, in Ingold, T., The Perception of the Environment, London & New York 2000, pp. 40–60, here: p. 47

is inscribed with the lives of all who have dwelt therein, from Distant Time human-animal ancestors to contemporary humans" (p. 54). It is exactly those places, for instance, designated as spiritual ones by Ingold, where vision quests take place. And places soaked of personal experience he mentions, are often places where daimonic epiphanies/visions occurred. (Cf. the article by Elke Mader[6], especially pp. 189-190: "In general, the relationships between man, nature and the supernatural are understood dynamically, in this structure the various areas are not sharply demarcated from each other, but interlocked. The different dimensions interact with each other and all beings undergo changes and transformations [...] The vision experience is at the centre of this dynamic." The Shuar and Achuar, Mader is talking about, do not supply and nourish themselves as hunters and gatherers only, they also practice slash-and-burn agriculture, p. 187.)

In this way point 5 and 6 would have become the new point I, and points 7-10 would be points II-V. And the question would arise: Where should/ could be points 1-4 located which you address? I would suggest they could be put as a parallel at point IV – in so far as they all could be subsumed under the category 'aesthetic access to nature' and this access historically emerges more or less simultaneously with the scientific access. That is: IV a: scientific; IV b: aesthetic.

The question of the turning point: nature – alienation II

With that if I am right, the question of the turning point arises completely anew. Where would the turning point be now? It may be positioned between II and III. And ipso facto some (romantic) premonition and hope would loom on the horizon: Could it be that if modern man succeeded to intensify and to deepen the aesthetic access to nature, he would come close to what Ingold called man-nature interagentivity – that he could transform nature alienation into nature friendship, distance towards nature into closeness to nature. It seems possible, which I hope I was able to make plausible in my presentation: „Naturästhetische Kontemplation und säkularisierte religiöse Naturerfahrung heute. Zum Beispiel 'Vision Quest'" ("Nature-aesthetic contemplation and secularised religious experience of nature today. For example 'Vision Quest'") dated April 9, 2016 in Rostock. Of course one

---

6   Elke Mader: Die Macht des Jaguars, in: Metamorphosen der Natur, ed. by A. Gingrich & E. Mader, Wien, Köln & Weimar 2002, pp. 183–222

could object here: "Oh boy, Kozljanič comes along with his vision quest again! Why can't he leave it at that?" Yes, I believe and hope that I can. And in this context I would like to point to David Abram's extraordinary book "The Spell of the Sensuous" (New York 1997). It is a glimmer of hope in many ways.

In a review of his book I wrote: He bridges his final and probably deepest thoughts with a Rilke poem by amalgamating images of bird, air, wind, and sky with those of the human soul and reason and thus outlining the sublime idea of an earth-born, enamoured of senses, and nature-loving reason; a reason that is sensually and corporally anchored and shows enough magnanimity to (re)award its soul to every natural place and every natural being.

»The human mind is not some otherworldly essence that comes to house itself inside our physiology. Rather, it is instilled and provoked by the sensorial field itself, induced by the tensions and participations between the human body and the animate earth. Invisible shapes of smells, rhythms of cricketsong, and the movements of shadows all, in a sense, provide the subtle body of our thoughts. Our own reflections, we might say, are a part of the play of light and *its* reflections. ›The inner – what is it, if not intensified sky?‹ [Rainer Maria Rilke] By acknowledging such links between the inner, psychological world and the perceptual terrain that surrounds us, we begin to turn inside-out, loosening the psyche from its confinement within a strictly human sphere, freeing sentience to return to the sensible world that contains us. Intelligence is no longer ours alone but is a property of the earth … Each place its own mind … Oak, madrone, Douglas fir, red-tailed hawk, serpentine in the sandstone, a certain scale to the topography, drenching rains in the winter, fog off-shore in the summer, salmon surging in the streams – all these together make up a particular state of mind, a place-specific intelligence shared by all the humans that dwell therein, but also … by all beings who live and make their way in that zone. Each place its own psyche. Each sky its own blue.« (p. 262.)

Reason that is so close to nature, indeed to place, can also take on a positive – ultimately a nature-poetic – task within our own written culture. We should, says Abram, lovingly and passionately take up our written language in order to re-adapt and inscribe it to the landscape.

»Our craft is that of releasing the budded, earthly intelligence of our words, freeing them to respond to the speech of the things themselves – to the green uttering-forth of leaves from the spring branches. It is the practice of spinning stories that have the rhythm and lilt of the local soundscape, tales for the tongue, tales that want to be told, again and again, sliding off the digital screen and slipping off the lettered page to inhabit these coastal forests, those desert canyons, those whispering grasslands and valleys and swamps.« (pp. 273-274)

Each sky – it's own blue

The liberating and unclosing principle of Abram's book is that he is serious about Nietzsche's ingenious postulation of pursuing the grand reason of the body – but without adopting his exaltations, resentments and hysterias of thinking. In doing so Abram orientates himself above all by the corporal phenomenology of Merleau-Ponty – like Nietzsche – not free from decadent dialectic socratisms and school-based philosophical sophisms. But Abram does not adhere to that! Why? This is because he rather trusts his body, his intuition and nature than the trends and conventions of academies. This is because he hangs around in nature and with people who live in close touch with nature rather than sitting at his desk. Abram is a (post)modern friend of nature, a non-decadent nature-bohemian. Deep inside he also could conserve and cultivate something the great reason of one's body cannot be possessed and lived without (as I developed elsewhere): namely a childlike, body close, sensuous and playful ego with a great heart. And this is a point you emphasize again and again, which comes off badly in my deliberations: What we need is not only a great and reasonable body, but also a lot of patience when dealing with places; we need familiarity, bonding and attachment to heart-warming natural places, the ones that open up depth.

It is quite obvious: We cannot completely escape the time and the zeitgeist we were born in. And yet: As long as humans – especially those who are civilisationally thrown off (nature) track and most of all (post) modern humans – are and remain masters of the simultaneity of the non-simultaneity there is hope that some time this simultaneity of the non-simultaneity does not have, as it often is the case, the effect of producing an alienation of nature but friendship with it; as a utopian past that breaks into the present or is longed for. What is essential at last is a viable, down to earth, romantic utopian dream. Thus we could modify Ernst Bloch's remark: 'which seems to everyone in childhood and in which no one has ever been: homeland'[7] into 'what seems to everyone in childhood, what some people see as a romantic premonition on the horizon, but where no Westerner has been since the Axial Age: homeland.'

In the hope of not having mistaken or over-intellectualized your unclosing 10-step outline I remain

with homelike-utopian kind regards

R. J. K.

P.S.

You once asked me about the essay with the heart-warming places. Did I send it to you? I don't think so, I am afraid. Here it is.

---

7   In German: "das allen in der Kindheit scheint und worin noch niemand war: Heimat", Ernst Bloch: Das Prinzip Hoffnung, vol. 3, Frankfurt a. M. 1973, p. 1628

P.P.S. June 3, 2016:

Now I have foregrounded the diachronic, historical considerations. However, a good deal of your approach was to attach great value to the synchronic, psychological context and process of experiencing and perception – and by doing so our present, personal nature experience outside our front door, which is possible for us contemporaries to experience any time. This faded into the background a bit, but I do hope just temporarily. For I think that we should dedicate to this psychological approach (maybe including the corporal dimension) some detailed consideration, for that reason alone to get the turning point out of its historical distance (from the Axial Age) and to analyse it more thoroughly where and how it makes itself perceptible in our days and our mental state. I may take you up on that later.

4.
Anyone Can Be a Cat

Rudolf Gaßenhuber   June 24, 2016

Dear Mr Kozljanič

your letter was a pleasure for me. Our exchange of ideas and feelings means enrichment for me. With great pleasure, I read your recommendation: Lame Deer/Erdoes "Tahca Ushte. Seeker of Visions. The Life of a Sioux Medicine Man" (New York 1972) What I learn from this? I am an American Indian in many ways, yet not completely so. The American Indian culture and religion is not a role model in all cases; the historic liberation from magic and wizardry certainly meant good progress. In our history, however, the baby was thrown out with the bath water and what remained was a world of de-deification followed by a purely material world. With the old magic and wizardry, some of the charm, enchantment and soul was lost. We would need an Enlightenment 2.0, Enlightenment about technological and scientific rationality and its adjustments.

I am an American Indian, a primordial American Indian; I start with experiencing prior to the adjustments of religion, priests, and shamans. I am Kaspar Hauser (1812-1833; a German youth who claimed to have grown up in the total isolation of a darkened cell), half an animal that always corporally, not merely optically perceives and interacts. I write out of this mode: "1. First Impression: Pleasure. You perceive the group, you like it, perhaps the nice and warm sun is shining on it, it invites you to sit, to lay down, to linger. You lie there chatting and resting." The sun is shining, the stone is warm, I lay down, I am a cat. I consider this quite ordinary, so nothing special about it, every child, each not too civilized person can understand and do that. Almost everyone can be a cat.

I sit or lie there, warmed by the sun and live within this scene. I do not start with an aesthetic (corporally distant Kantian) experience, a mere delight. This scene is not a picture I am confronted with, I am part of it like the rock, the bug and the earthly smell.

I did not make it clear enough. It was too obvious to me. You reformulate the point into: "First pleasant, aesthetic experiencing and acquaintance of a place, a group of rocks (e.g. Álfastein prior to any type of construction)."

This is not what I meant to say, and this enables me to express myself more thoroughly. So I start as a primordial American Indian. The spirit of this place is warming and pleasant. It is the same or a similar spirit that a cat or a lizard can enjoy. – The warm stone – This spirit has no name, it is not even called "sun".

Are there any primordial American Indians? Is there any pre-religious, 'uncivilized' feeling? Yes, I think so, and it is more ordinary than we think. To a certain degree, every sound human is a "master of the simultaneity of the non-simultaneity", as you write so trenchantly. More things unite us humans than we think; indigenous peoples included. The great distance that has been readily created since the Age of Enlightenment (Kant, Herder) is a chimaera. St. Boniface can leave his church. Rather than on a cultural constant, modernity is based on a permanent effort, a permanent training of distancing, which is endangered by failure at all times; the beach lies under the pavement; underneath technology lies the togetherness of souls.

In Tahca Ushte's book I found two nice passages I would like to bring to your attention in order to outline the whole idea. "My mother died of tubercolosis in 1920, when I was seventeen years old, and that was our family's 'last stand.' … I was holding her hand and she was looking at me … She said, '*Onsika, onsika* – pitiful, pitiful.' These were her last words. … For four days I felt my mother's *nagi*, her presence, her soul, near me. I felt that some of her goodness was staying with me. The priest talked about eternity. I told him we Indians did not believe in a forever and forever. We say that only the rocks and the mountains last, but even they will disappear." (p. 37)

For me this is a very touching passage. The spirit, 'spiritus', the soul are addressed as goodness and rendered here in all its liveliness and reality. These are not ghosts or eternal souls. There is the bond with his mother, her radiance, her smile. Her goodness is present. Her goodness was 'always' there for her child – but it was not eternal.

For Christians their leader is present on Whitsuntide in this way, at least it was so at the beginning. Today hardly nobody knows it; we just run around and carry out any type of actions which may lead to situational devotion, but do not mean Whitsuntide. Here we can see the disloyal distance of any reified religiosity. Tahca Ushte is a primordial American Indian in many ways, and here he is particularly gratifying to me. In many other aspects, however, even American Indians are not spared these fixations. This is an exciting, deep topic:

The distance from the phenomenal, nature-close, animal-like experiencing. I am writing 'animal-like' and try to avoid the negative associations that are associated with all terms in this field: beastly, animalistic, also bestial. What I mean is an immediate and unbroken experience, which everybody can see when watching animals. A mouse is a mouse is a mouse. Experiencing and existence and action, a circular Feedback Circle (Jakob von Uexküll) are closely intertwined. The human condition means to distinguish oneself 'more or less' from this animal-like existence due to a conscious past, a private world and future. In this 'more or less' lies the doleful outcry, as the saying goes, of our species and our cultural history.

And a sparrow is a sparrow
is a sparrow

Let us go back to Tahca Ushte and my second favourite passage. It equally examines the difference between phenomenal and cultural. In the chapter on the sun dance the necessary actions and ritual objects as well as cruel acts are described that constitute a good and true sun dance. In the text the atmosphere is very tense and marked by anxious care; thousands of taboos could be broken thousands of things could go awry. It is really surprising, and I am finally surprised about the name "sun dance", because the sun is so generous and providing us with unconditioned warmth. So why is there such petty, anxious concern? Has it always been the case or is this anxiousness part of the cultural junk that encrusts our souls?

We know about Whitsuntide, for instance, that once disciples came together in 'his spirit' and his spirit was present then, simply a successful revival. But what are the roots of the sun dance? I don't know whether sources and texts exist to this end. But Tahca Ushte has a suspicion, and I can well imagine that to be more accurate: "The sun dance is our oldest and most solemn ceremony … It is so old that its beginnings are hiden as in a mist. … I think the Indians knew the sun and the moon much better in those long-forgotten days, were much closer to them [than today's scientists]." And now Tahca Ushte describes the first sun dance, as it were – how it could have taken place: "Huddling in their poor shelters in the darkness of winter, freezing and hungry, hibernating almost like animals, how joyfully, thankfully they must have greeted the life-giving sun … I can imagine one of them on a sudden impulse getting up to dance for the sun, using his body like a prayer …" (p. 199) Yes, it goes well together, this is a sun dance that deserves its name, a dance based on the joy and thankfulness for the spring sun. (But were the conditions really so miserable?)

The following sentence is unwillingly rather unmasking: "So they made this dance, and slowly, generation after generation, added more meaning to it, added to its awesomeness" (p. 199). The dance was awe-inspiring and not the sun. Joy and thankfulness are no longer experiences as such but the rite increasingly occupies the experience. They concentrate on things, actions and self-induced pain; sun and spring fall into oblivion. It starts here.

My point 1) was conceived in this way, as a first perception, first joy, as a pre-cultural, animal-like feeling. The spiritual is also present here: as joy, as thankfulness, as kindness. In point 5) a "certain assumption of an independent reality/specification of spirits (and the spiritual)" appears as you call it. Or more simply, goodness becomes the eternal soul, the dance of joy becomes a rite. The spirit turns into spirits and rites. Any immediate experience is phenomenal, is 'spiritual', in any case some experience. This also applies for the modern human. The dominant ideology of constructivism/materialism is only one layer of this idea, which is not part of the authentic experience. For instance I address a couple saying: "When sitting together side by side and appose your heads, then you can feel a flow and closeness." The woman's spontaneous answer is: "But this sounds pretty esoteric." I say: "Yes – but it feels like that." As a rule, I do not have to add anything. Bent back on our own feeling the dead haunting crumbles away. Or I speak about inner voices (e.g. conscience), house spirits (e.g. house and relationship atmosphere) or the famous expression 'trouble's brewing'. I have never observed that someone does not understand it. On the contrary, I often have the impression of relief: at last something may be named I have always experienced. You are certainly right when saying ghosts are not (officially accepted) as part of our modern western world. But this only pertains at best to the childhood faith of ghostly incarnation. As mentioned before, if we speak about a good house spirit or team spirit or about atmospheres and moods we do not receive any resistance. But you are right in so far as this layer of personal feeling is forced back and what remains is a distant view and distant action. The feeling of togetherness with others and with oneself is vestigial, largely discontinued. Otherwise the world would not look like as it is. Therefore people seek therapy: the destructive cultural layer made of fear, mistrust duty, loneliness, the hate of anything weak has grown too thick, there is an erosion of resources concerning basic trust, being loved, and meaningfulness, life often tends to result in an inner death.

Trenchantly formulated, the whole point of therapy, for instance, is to uncover the primordial American Indian, his basic trust in himself and the world and make them grow. When I think about it, my role model for this process is not indigenous peoples but animals, closeness to nature, greater proximity towards us, non-schizophrenic experiencing. Where would we find that for sure if not among animals? Lately I stood in front of the chimpanzee house in Nuremberg again, for a couple therapist this is a dream of liveliness: Easy changes between closeness and distance, emotional security, aggression, hierarchy everything is integrated here and in motion, nothing stagnates and seethes.

So I join your postscript from the following day: We should retrieve the turning point from its historic distance and examine where and how it makes itself noticeable. It is my deep conviction that we are mentally closer to the indigenous peoples than most people think, and that we are closer connected with animals than most people think (and must think).

Meta criticism

On second perusal I wonder, which turn the chain of thought has taken. Owing to Tahca Ushte it became very clear to me that distance towards nature has not been a topic since the Neolithic Age only but a topic pertaining to humanity in general to a different degree. Certainly, 'indigenous peoples' are much more closely intertwined with nature and much closer to it directly, but the immediacy of experiencing is broken unlike that of animals. Consisting of interpretations and myths, spirits and rites, a layer spreads out over the immediate world of experiencing.

The result is surprising to me, because we have always known it that human beings are cultural beings who almost always and almost necessarily interpose their own worlds between themselves and reality. This division between experiencing I (animal-like, human) and experiencing II (civilised, human) distinguishes all humans. It was not until Rousseau and romanticism that 'indigenous' peoples were invented and deeply rooted into the present as role models and an antithesis. They certainly are exemplary in many ways. But if we look out for "closeness to nature", "friendship with nature", an end towards "alienation", we have to free ourselves from Rousseau and watch more carefully. A hint in the direction of indigenous peoples is not enough.

But where do we find a criterion for that? What does closeness to nature mean, where is the goal? I liked your nice and meaningful outline on David Abram and the subsequent airy extension about patience, familiarity, and attachment. Thus we have three possible sources of closeness to nature: A) mystic identification, B) poetry and C) attachment. This is quite a lot. To my mind three further sources add to them: D) nature knowledge literally beginning with Seneca until Goethe (hence prior to the 'cold-hearted and objective' science), E) life within nature and F) visions, trances, dreams, daydreams. Some remarks on this:

Ad A) Mystic identification (Averroism)

A nice, real hint on this is to be found in Tahca Ushte's book (thank you again for this reference!): "The buffalo was part of us, his flesh and blood being absorbed by us until it became our own flesh and blood. Our clothing, our tipis, everything we needed for life came from the buffalo's body. It was hard to say where the animal ended and the man began." Hence there are not only sensuous, aesthetic, poetic fusions, inductions, and resonances, but also a process of exchange in fundamental life. This connection is existential, it lacks any modern consumer attitude: "When the buffalo disappeared, the old, wild Indian disappeared too." (p. 255). The unity with nature is also realized in the real way of life.

Ad B) Poetry, feeling for nature ...

Ad C) Attachment

Attachment constitutes something unique in view of 'this one' in his/her uniqueness. There is a relationship and connection with much and everything in his own way like in your quotation by Abram: "Each place its own psyche. Each sky its own blue." This is appreciative and appreciating, but with flexible ties. Places string together, all possess something distinct and estimable, we can have a connection with all of them, we virtually stroll through the world and have an experience. You rightly establish the association with the bohemian, the independent artist. Today this attitude goes well with the mobile, flexible employee who is expected to be able to settle fast and well in any place anew. In your beautiful article on heart-warming places ("Such places partake of something warm in a way.") this is the main type of the places in question, I think. Another type of attachment to places is more fateful and existential. Your attachment to the maple alley in the Limesstraße is part of your irretrievable biography like the place of birth and place of death. Many, many places embrace something irretrievable and unique in place and time. Among indigenous peoples, the whole world consists of such non-exchangeable places. They are heart-warming, appealing but also fateful. I think about the Black Hills or the Pipestone National Monument in Minnesota. These places are of an almost infinite importance for these peoples. They risk their life for them. In Dee Brown's book "Bury my Heart at Wounded Knee" we can witness this terrible fight for their holy places. If we read that, we must feel ashamed in multiple ways to be white men.

Ad D) Nature knowledge

Hunters and gatherers possess an excellent knowledge about their flora and fauna. Even today a good deal of our drugs is derived from plant extracts – but people do not know it any more. If the drug helps us we gladly thank, inside of us, the physician or the pharmacist but not the herb. Modern humans prefer staying among their own kind. – And every lab drug is based on natural resources and with its entire necessary societal complexity on a well functioning ecology, for instance on the Limacina helicina known as the sea butterfly, a tiny beginning of the food chain. Do we know about its beauty and have we ever expressed it our gratitude?[1]

Sea butterflies are among the endangered species in polar waters

Ad *E) Life within nature*

Indigenous peoples live much closer to nature; the layers of technical procedures are much thinner. To my mind, the way of life must be a distinct point in the list of factors dealing with closeness to nature. Let us briefly think of the Plains Indians. Since 1890 (Wounded Knee) there have been no more free tribes. But back then what was life like, the sense of life and the feeling of being in the world – without a state, as a small sovereign group depending for better or worse on regional, natural resources? The buffalo and the American Indian were the same being, the forest was the parents elsewhere. Ingold calls it the "quality of a close relationship" that constitutes "interagentivity". What shall this quirky word mean? He probably means parental love, plus care, plus dependence, plus exchange, plus attachment,

---

1   http://dw.com/deco2-im-meer-gefährdet-fische-und-korallen/a-17259997

plus identity. The American Indians 'are' the buffalo, the archaic forest dwellers 'are' the woods. A grand freedom and a close attachment go hand in hand here. – This life as a free tribe in nature is no longer possible for us today. But the dependency still exists, it is just less regional, less directly visible and no longer perceived in feelings and concepts of kinship.

Ad *F) Visions, trances, dreams, daydreams*

My understanding of dreams is feelings translated into pictures. We think in a particular way when dreaming; it is a way of thinking by means of feelings that unfolds and expresses itself in pictures. Joy, anxiety, worries, and all kinds of outstanding accounts during the day make up a nucleus that can rise to great stories. The dream also looks for solutions within the stories. We repeatedly dream about the same topic in one night moving from one solution to the other. In life and the mental development of a person dreams play a fundamental role. Without this second way of thinking life does not properly evolve. But equally as the conscious way of thinking, the second one is not infallible either. These are attempts, new outlines enabling the dreamer and the thinker to move a great step forward.

These are not infallible or unalterable revelations. – I would classify visions in the same way. What do you think?

Third process – what should we do?

How can we reduce alienation and the distance towards nature? If animals are the better role model and not indigenous peoples – how can humans find a decent life? A human cannot become an animal and not a free American Indian or an archaic forest dweller either. Many compromises remain with us: Animal love, love for a place, mysticism, mindfulness, addressability, nature knowledge, also encounters, and trances within nature ... Simply put: allow what is. Goodness is goodness and not an eternal soul; the spring sun we experience is warming, powerful, redeeming, not a solar deity, and not an "average sized star at the outer third of the Milky Way" – first phrase in the German Wikipedia article on the sun. – (So far-fetched is the widespread opinion on it already; our perceptiveness and attention are caged in a prison made of theories and thoughts. It is not until the last Wikipedia paragraph on the cultural history (!) of the sun, where a reference to life on earth is to be found: "The sun is the central celestial body, every life form depends on it.

Ever since humans were aware of its phenomenal importance." What does it mean, if this phrase is not to be found at the beginning?)

Last but not least, two remarks:

Dionysus

"Affirmative loyalty, Dionysian concern and life under the sun", this sounds beautiful, and it should happen soon. "Exploited of all countries show solidarity!" – Brothers, depart, rise up to the sun, to freedom! ... However, I fear that humanity has been in a state of departure for far too long. Since ancient times and even before and the more so since the Renaissance humans have been devoted to growth and progress. Well, can the departure itself be the problem? Thus the circle was opened and bent to a line, the self-determined future was invented. (We should not forget Claude Lévi-Strauss and his "cold and hot cultures".)

Nietzsche or Camus, are they for the topic of closeness, love, family, integration good authorities? I don't think so. Both had great difficulties in this respect. Both grew up under a subtle or open tyranny of violent women. Camus grew up without his father, but he had a devoted and anxious mother; his grandmother whipped him regularly and his loving mother accepted it. "The First Man" means some agonizing wrestling until hate breaks out of him, and he ".... one day, suddenly furious with rage and violence, snatched the bullwhip from her hand and was so determined to strike that white head whose cold, bright eyes drove him to frenzy ..."[2]. Here, a first man was made out of a Nothing – out of a world in which love had always been linked to weakness. An unattached, isolated hunger for life, "a single, ever-vibrating blade, as it were" (p. 239) wrests from miserable and stupid conditions. For Camus it was an important step and a great awakening towards grand literature.

And when transferring it to humanity, what does it mean? To put it slangily, this will not work. The beginning cannot be violence and coldness; justified anger can be an important ferment, but never a basis. This is why I believe that Nietzsche and Camus are mirrors and relay racers of their time: Violence creates departure, creates sundries ... And this is the reason why I like your Tahca Ushte so much, he still represents something of the old

---

2   Albert Camus: Der erste Mensch, Reinbek 1995, p. 232

cyclical Great Spirit, some of that earthiness and silent obviousness. – And when taking a closer look, you will notice that the mood is not a departure but an attempt: "We must try to use the pipe for mankind, which is on the road to self-destruction." I find this magnificent and moving. I think this is the only way even if it were without any success. It goes on to say: "We must try to get back on the red road of the pipe, the road of life. … This can be done only if all of us, Indians and non-Indians alike, can again see ourselves as part of this earth, not as an enemy from the outside who tries to impose its own will on it" (pp. 265-266). Brilliant and profound this casual insertion "from outside"! This is the core of it, the pronounced counterpart, the absence of being part of it. Metaphorically speaking the salvation could not result from a march with fanfares and drums but at best from a circle where we smoke a pipe and "form again the circle without end" (p. 266).

Your presentation: Nature-aesthetic contemplation

It is a very subtle, delicate implementation avoiding any sort of deterrence to the topic of visions. I particularly savoured the citations "when taking a closer look burgeoning life everywhere. The desert after the rain! I am full of great joy." – I do not know whether it is appropriate to call it a "pantheistic feeling", in any case, there is great joie de vivre – joyful, connected, and redeeming. – I do not quite understand the position of this experiencing in the context of your presentation. The aim of your presentation seems to be the rediscovery of the "seriousness of religious authority" in modern vision quests as well. The serious quest of religious origins in the Numinous of Rudolf Otto and Hermann Schmitz, however, it leads to a melange of shiver and fascination. Are these not two divergent concepts about the origin of religion, once awe and fear, once joy and attachment? The experiencing you mention, does it not contradict the concept of seriousness and any hierarchic understanding of religion? Did it arise a debate? Earlier Sloterdijk advocated a hedonistic, joyful-mystic position in his "Critique of Cynical Reason"; did he approach Schmitz? How was Rostock, did your presentation go down well?

Well, it has been a long letter now with quite a lot of topics. Take what you find appealing. I will be glad to hear from you again.

Kind regards

R. G.

Robert J. Kozljanič   July 29, 2016

Dear Mr Gaßenhuber

More than one month has gone by, and my answer is long overdue. But I do not only appreciate our exchange of thoughts but also enjoy it very much – that is why I only can/wish to answer when having a bit of leisure – enabling me to go intellectually into depth and allowing one or the other philosophical idea melt in my mouth.

At the moment, the lecture series "Fathers and Mothers of the Philosophy of Life" conceived by Dr. Elke Wachendorff and myself as part of the Nietzsche-Forum München as well as the final editing and the layout of the 8th Yearbook for Philosophy of Life (topic: "Kritik und Therapie wissenschaftlicher Unvernunft" – "Critique and Therapy of Scientific Irrationality") absorb all my excess capacity. So may I ask you for a little patience?

I equally wanted to tell you about my idea which has been growing for some time in the back of my head: What do you think of completing and bringing our correspondence to a result – let's say by the end of the year – in order to publish it? [...] As for me, this correspondence is very particular, it has a dialogic quality and a constant reference to experience, which I often sadly miss elsewhere. And I think that the topics we approach definitely are of some general importance and general interest. What do you think?

Kind regards

R. J. K.

Rudolf Gaßenhuber   July 31, 2016

Dear Mr Kozljanič

thank you, you cannot ask more nicely for patience. There is no need to hurry. I would gladly back the publication of our correspondence.

A few things, nevertheless, should be revised. In my last letter, for instance, I termed the science of the post Goethe era as heart-cold, 'objective' science. These two adjectives should be both put in inverted commas: 'heart-cold, objective' science, because it is not generally heart-cold. Science and technology are decidedly Janus-faced phenomena – often helpful and furthering humans for a short time, but destructive for nature in the long run. With the help of them humans, like almost no other species, have spread extremely successfully over the entire globe. Technology is helpful and life saving. And any expansion of boundaries, like genetic engineering as an example, with its principal and often factual life-saving potential is emotionally praised. But success and calamity are closely entangled. What do you think?

Well, we probably won't run short of topics. But nevertheless it seems feasible to think of "completing and bringing our correspondence to a result". I'd be glad to.

I wish you still pleasant summer weeks

Kind regards

R. G.

P.S.: I'd be glad to read your philosophy of life yearbook and am hereby ordering it.

5

OPENING AND CULTIVATING THE SENSE OF HEART

Robert J. Kozljanič   January 12, 2017

Dear Mr Gaßenhuber

finally indeed, I've found the time to answer you. Back until February I have now read and reread for (re-)thinking and (again and again for the sake of self-scrutinizing) our fascinating and inspiring correspondence. With great pleasure and inner enrichment I also read your last longer letter dated June 24, 2016. In this letter you succeed – openly and honestly – to summarize many a topic discussed beforehand. I'd definitely have, of course, to add some critical remarks in detail (It is not for nothing that I am a philosopher ;-) And I will do so subsequently. But I do not intend to foreground criticism now. There is and should be something else for me in the foreground, it is a basic feeling. And this feeling tells me: How philosophically lovely and consistently, how humanly (in an 'animal-like humanly' as well as in a 'cultivated humanly' sense) and true-to-life you grasped many things we discussed and got to the heart of them! A further discussion and a restart of new topics wouldn't it be like dissolving and talking these topics to death? Does not our own intellect have an urgently wanting and compulsive character? In so far as, after an extended and productive discussion, we feel that all crucial things have been fully differentiated, verbalized, explained and summarized, we then tend to 'lay back' somehow reassured and content; that we are sated (*lt.: satis facere – do enough; satisfactio – satisfaction*) not in a crude (or lazy) sense but in a simple sense. And then sometimes, faster than we hope for, we get hungry for new questions. This again could certainly be a (mental and very intellectual) way to close a circle – to round off something – round off provisionally – and to 'leave it at that'; until a next circle of questions opens and comes to the fore.

If I still have quite a few things to tell hereafter, I hope that it does not have the character of discussing it to death but of a mutual rounding off. This is at least my sincere wish.

First some points of criticism – and then a few words on my Rostock presentation.

Critique: Why Rousseau is indispensable despite all that

You say that we must detach ourselves from Rousseau and his 'indigenous peoples' model/antithesis. It remains an open question whether and how it is possible to do. You do replace the 'indigenous people-like' principle by the 'animal-like' one. But to me it seems to be the same concept as Rousseau's – to paraphrase it: a quite similar 'back to nature' idea – including all possible and impossible ways of such 'back'. It shows that, for certain contexts, we simply cannot move away from the Rousseauian model/antithesis – and maybe it is not reasonable to free oneself from it. I believe that Rousseau described and promoted quite an important concept. Herder advanced a bit further on this way. Both tried to interpret humans on the basis of their own history of civilization and nature – within nature and out of nature. Both tried to interpret humans rather from their biological, psychological, historical origins and thus to direct them away from the civilizing alienation from nature. And both were inspired by the belief that intrinsically nature is good – and thus the very first nature of humans; misinterpretations and drawbacks add afterwards through a societal process of oppression and superstructure and strategic power calculation. Thus both of them have provided powerful and efficacious arguments for the criticism of civilization. This remains to be acknowledged. In my view your 'error in reasoning' is that you thought the 'nature-based condition' tendentially refers to the past. But when taking a closer look, this 'nature-based condition' contains at least as much presence and future like past and prehistory. Finally – and this is shown in Herder's "Briefen zu Beförderung der Humanität" – the nature-based condition is a dynamic and sustainable ideal which enables a discussion what to keep from the past about '(good) nature' and what not! And how we want to work together on a coherent nature and human friendly concept for our future. Perhaps we cannot talk about a 'nature-based condition' without becoming too utopian. If it were so: Would it be bad? I do not think so.

It would rather further a more conscious efficiency process in handling utopian ideas, would turn u-topian ideas (in the literal sense of the word meaning non-topian ideas or ideas of non-existent places) into rather future-topian ideas, future-places …

My Rostock Presentation: Aesthetic Devotion and Religious Seriousness

As shown in my Rostock presentation on "Naturästhetische Kontemplation" (nature aesthetic contemplation), the (post)modern vision quest frequently reaches a depth of experiencing where "aesthetic enjoyment" changes into "aesthetic devotion" and ultimately into "aesthetic religion". – My presentation was well received in two respects. The rather nature-loving 'folks' were highly enthusiastic that there finally is someone who voices something they had been thinking about and experienced for themselves, a circumstance that normally remains unspoken. The rather academically socialised and purely intellectual 'guys' were not really appalled, but somehow bemused – especially about the ease and authenticity of my speech about contemporary aesthetic and aesthetically-religious experiencing and experiences. They tried to rationalize the seemingly spiritual phenomena of experiencing I had described.

The subsequent statements materialized in a naïvely rationalistic and 'droll' way. Sometimes I have to ask myself: Why are these overly intellectual people unable of leaving such experiencing as it is: lively experienced and processed into real life experiences? (You addressed this point as well, and I will come back to it soon. – And anyway: There was a majority of conference individuals who were talking and sitting, who only existed intellectually and cognitively so to speak. At some time or another this "body-distant" sedentary way was too much for me. So I skipped some presentations, backed out for a couple of hours and drove to the near beach of the Baltic Sea. Although it was not really warm, I had to get a bit in touch with the sea with all my senses. I took off my fine trousers and bathed my feet in the sand and the water; see images).

The Baltic Sea. Beach near Rostock & My feet greet the Baltic Sea

Herrmann Schmitz himself was neither bemused nor highly enthusiastic about my presentation. He uttered that I had presented a new type of "nature religion" (in quotation marks). But he doubted whether we could speak of religion or religious devotion in the strict sense of the word. He pointed out that, to his mind, the description of my atmospheres and experiencing lacked the "authority" of "absolute earnestness", this (life-)groundbreaking aspect which underlies any religious experience. I did not contradict him right away (it would have been too confrontational in this context) albeit these were exactly the elements I had brought forward in my examples of experience that had clearly been presented, in my opinion. Nonetheless I stuck to my guns (this is my way) and reminded him politely in a certain manner, which is normally known of him, with a citation from his own "System der Philosophie" (vol. 3.4, p. 641) where he definitely conceded transitory fields between both types of devotion (religious and aesthetic). And my clear intention was to point to these transitory fields. With this in mind, the discussion ended barren of results. Of course, I could have hinted again at the last examples of experience I had quoted[1]. These were examples of unmistakable visionary and life-determining experiencing, which always appeared, N.B., within the framework of a "personal religion" (William James) and as an experience of "absolute earnestness" or they were at least partly charged with considerable authority; an authority which they did not owe to the mercy of clerical, political or scientific institutions. The issue here was an individual and existential authority, which might result from the boundary experience itself. I deliberately speak of a boundary experience. And boundary experiences can be earnest, very earnest indeed – and partly

---

1   From the book by Steven Foster and Meredith Little: Vision Quest, Sinnsuche und Selbstheilung in der Wildnis, Braunschweig 1991, p. 90

threatening and can drive you to the verge of madness. And it is this boundary experience of the individual in question that demonstrates the earnestness and life-determining authority – but only for the one who is individually concerned.

But I readily admit that it is a matter of transitory phenomena and overlapping fields and not of identical ones. And it also means that there are many fields where the "earnestness of religious authority" of collectivist cultures and/or dogmatically repressive religions does not overlap with the rather individual (and sometimes by nature less severe) earnestness of a "personal religion" and a personally aesthetic devotion – obviously not.

Religious earnestness and 'deadly earnestness ', devotion and laughter

What becomes clear is: Schmitz' critique moved in the same direction as yours – concerning the "earnestness of religious authority" in modern vision quest experiencing. Together with R. Otto and Schmitz – you associate "earnestness of religious authority" imperatively with shudder, fascination, awe, and fear. But such a strictly compelling association only pertains, in my opinion to patriarchic and, according to Ruth Benedict ("Patterns of Culture", New York 1934), "Apollonian" religions, which often have and need at the same time a strict, punitive, angry, avenging God the Father. But it is not true of many indigenous cultures and religions (in particular, this does not apply to the "Dionysian" religions/cultures). Here, even among the most 'earnest' ones, a spontaneous fit of laughter is always possible. There are fascinating examples of ethnographic literature and the literature of expeditions and adventure trips. I witnessed again and again when the Lakota shaman Elmer Norbert Running (Rosebud Reservation, South Dakota) was heartily joking during healing and sweat lodge ceremonies. Religious earnestness and a hearty laughter were closely connected here and were not contradictory. Here are two examples: There was this seminar week in Switzerland organized by the Munich sweat lodge group, of which I was a long-standing member and co-founder. We had invited Elmer and his former wife Patti (from the Santee-Sioux Reservation in North Nebraska) as well as one nephew to an isolated farm in the middle of nature in a deep river valley – on a hot early summer day. And when the fireman brought in the glowing rocks into the so-called sweat lodge – which is rather an igloo-like sweat tent and not a lodge – it got really hot then. Finally the tent flap was closed. About 15 people were present in this small sweat tent. It was pretty crowded and hot. It was completely dark inside except for the magic of the red-hot stones in the middle. And before Elmer started singing and pouring water over the heated rocks he told a story, a story to show us, as he said, the immense power of the Lakota sweat lodge. So it once occurred that an elderly, hampered man begged for healing by a Lakota sweat lodge. And then it happened, when the fireman carried the red-hot rocks inside one after the other. One rock slipped off from the fork and rolled directly between this old man's legs. "And", Elmer finished his story, "what do you think, how fast this man got healed? And how fast he was seen running?" – When Elmer had finished this story there was a silence for about five seconds.

There was an embarrassed silence. Until it suddenly dawned on us that Elmer's story was simply a joke. No one expected the Lakota shaman to be joking in such a religious and emotionally charged ritual situation. We did not expect it in the context of such a ceremony, hence the embarrassed silence. And then the first participants caught on to it and exploded with laughter. Then the whole tent was filled with roaring laughter. Interestingly this laughter dissolved the forced spiritual atmosphere often to be watched when (we) Westerners 'practice' religion or spirituality. And this dissolving and relaxing effect was anything but detrimental to the subsequent sweat lodge experience we had. On the contrary: It was one of the most intensive – also prayer intensive – sweat lodge experiences I have ever had.

Sweat lodge

In the evening after sunset, the Lowampi healing ceremony took place. It is held in a spacious, secluded and absolutely dark room. The Lowampi healing ceremony is the 'little brother' of the Yuwipi healing ceremony (which you already know from the Tahca Ushte book). On the whole it is quite similar, but unlike during the Yuwipi healing ceremony the shaman is not fettered. At the beginning of the said Lowampi ceremony and shortly before Elmer and his nephew the drummer and singer called in the spirits, Elmer said to us: "Now watch out! When the spirits enter me while healing through me, then I am often beside myself. And then I can see quite well despite the darkness. I can see upon you from one corner of the room's ceiling, for instance. Therefore: Do not pick your nose, I see that, too!" – If you do remember, Tahca Ushte reports quite similar incidents from his Yuwipi ceremonies: When the spirits enter him while healing through him, then he is often beside himself. I described it in my book "Kunst und Mythos" ("Art and Myth") as ecstasy-enstasy linkage: While the spirits are inside the shaman's body and heal through him, the shaman is often beside himself, this means that he is outside his body – which sometimes involves an 'heautoscopy' experience (out-of-body experience with autoscopy).

All this shows me that there is no such deadly earnestness among these down-to-earth religions, and they are less ideological in comparison with superstructure religions (e.g. during Catholic or Protestant rites). This 'deadly earnestness' is rather our cup of tea. In order to secure his above-mentioned arguments Hermann Schmitz revealingly pointed to such 'deadly earnest' religious situations in his church attendance experiences as a child.

Unobstructed joy and pantheistic feeling

One last remark concerning my Rostock presentation: You asked whether it "is good" to speak of a pantheistic feeling in connection with the experience of "being filled with great joy" expressed by quester Iris? You only pointed to the first quotation ("… I am filled with great joy"); obviously because it came the closest to what you outlined earlier as 'simply an animal-like-being creature within nature'. You did not mention, however, the second more important passage (together with the quotation). It read: "For Iris it is the desert that evokes the pantheistic experiencing. In her diary she wrote down the following words by the Tuareg nomad Mano Dayak. 'For me the desert is extraordinarily beautiful and pure, concurrently shocking and adorable. Each time I am confronting HER, SHE leads me to the exciting voyage into my own ego, where wistful memories, concerns and hopes of life struggle with each other. It was the desert which taught me the dialogue with the mystery of infinity.' These words, said Iris, 'which I read and reread, summarize so densely what I feel.'" Well: Both Iris and Mano Dayak have a 'dialogue with the mystery of infinity.'

A dialogue initially felt by Iris before she finds words for it – with Mano Dayak. I don't consider the term "pantheistic feeling" so inappropriate. And if you look at the examples submitted by William James in his "The Varieties of Religious Experience" (New York 1902) under the keyword "cosmic consciousness" (pp. 385–391), you will see that James assesses it similarly. As I mention in my book on friendship with nature under point 5.3.1.[2], a contemporary deep ecologist, Timothy Sprigge, sees it likewise. "It is, according to Sprigge, the feeling connecting us, at least in some cases, with 'natural objects' and which suggests that the 'character, which they mean for us to have, can [also] exist independently of us'. 'The views we are offered by a lonely scenery and the feelings connected with it or the sea hitting vividly against the cliffs convey a feeling of oneness with nature, which is not an illusion to my mind'." – But here I don't want to insist dogmatically neither. But here the question remains as well: Where does the feeling end in the case of a pantheistic experience and something else gains importance? Let's say cognitive moments of a modern knowledge about the infinity of the universe, knowledge that is vertiginous per se and which turns again into some sort of a feeling – a vertigo feeling. Or the question remains – this was your request, I think – whether such experiencing always has to be entitled as "pantheistic" and by doing so produce a verbal overload. Simply, don't do that except for this: "I am filled with great joy"? Yes, you are right. Sometimes we should leave it at this great joy – without talking too much. Angelus Silesius put it so nicely: "The rose blossoms without knowing why, heedless of itself, oblivious to our eye." And this is exactly the way our joy should be able to blossom prior to all philosophical questioning and controversy. Here again you have stricken a chord. It is a point that leads close to the "sense of heart" (more of that below)...

---

2   Robert Josef Kozljanič: Freundschaft mit der Natur – Naturphilosophische Praxis und Tiefenökologie, Klein Jasedow 2008, p. 105

Then concerning your question whether Sloterdijk got closer to Schmitz? – I do not believe it. And yet they were always very close about certain topics. The strongest of them certainly is the "atmospheric" topic (cf. the chapter on the "anthropic climate" in P. Sloterdijk "Globes"[3], where he sparsely but distinctly quotes Schmitz).

Attempt of a mutual rounding

Yet I want finally come to a rounding. You wrote: "If animals are the better role model and not indigenous peoples – how can humans find a decent life? A human cannot become an animal and not a free American Indian or an archaic forest dweller either." So our question remains with your own words: "How can we reduce alienation and the distance towards nature?" And further on: "Many compromises remain with us: Animal love, love for a place, mysticism, mindfulness, addressability, nature knowledge, also encounters, and trances within nature ... Simply put: allow what is. Goodness is goodness and not an eternal soul; the spring sun we experience is warming, powerful, redeeming, not a solar deity, and not an 'average sized star at the outer third of the Milky Way' [...]."

And in this or a quite similar sense I also mentioned in my book "Friendship with Nature" the "ability of leaving nature as it is", as a key competence of a practical philosophy of nature that is fundamental for all particular types and practices connecting us with nature respectively intending to escape our distance and alienation from nature[4]. Or as I wrote in my presentation "Vision und Verantwortung" ("Vision and Responsibility"): "The access to nature is primarily realised when something 'is left alone', without any distraction of perception, but a serene orientation towards the free nature. Let yourself and nature simply be. And therefore – only therefore – the proper and the 'other' nature, free as it is, can become evident. All those who have ever tried it know that practising this 'leave it alone' attitude is not easy at all. There are countless examples of people when having really stayed outdoors alone and undistracted, did not know how to deal with it, and they reacted with neurotic compulsive acts: They were compulsively busy doing or changing anything. If you have ever experienced such a thing,

---

3   Peter Sloterdijk: Globes. Spheres Volume II: Macrospherology, Cambridge, Massachusetts 2014

4   Robert Josef Kozljanič: Freundschaft mit der Natur, Klein Jasedow 2008, pp. 56-57.

you know what is going on here. The habitually well organized targeted and purposeful thoughts suddenly circle restlessly and erratically in your head. The busy desire of change is too deeply rooted in our modern way of life. The ability of leaving it alone – staying calm and not intervening is a rare commodity, which must be acquired by the civilised man anew. In general terms I think that in the nature-philosophical and practical context (as well as in experiential education of nature) learning about the 'leave it alone' attitude should be in first place."[5]

Access to the sources of life

What is confusing me about your above-mentioned words is that you wrote under the heading "Third process – what should we do?": "Many compromises remain with us". Are we really talking about compromising? Are these compromises? Should we content ourselves with compromises concerning such a central issue? I am inwardly reluctant against it (speaking with Socrates: my "Daimonion" is reluctant). As mentioned further above your first formulation does not read 'compromises' but 'sources'. "Thus we have three possible sources of closeness to nature: A) mystic identification, B) poetry and C) attachment. This is quite a lot. To my mind three further sources add to them: D) nature knowledge literally beginning with Seneca until Goethe (hence prior to the 'cold-hearted and objective' science), E) life within nature and F) visions, trances, dreams, daydreams." When talking about "sources" my Daimonion calms down. This word fits much better, in my opinion. This is at least the word I use, when speaking of sources or life sources when addressing these or similar contexts. These sources are free and complimentary and are like gushing springs: They constantly throw themselves away on you. The only problem (for us over-civilized, over-engineered, over-consuming, over-productive humans) is to find them, to get an access to them. For this access is mostly heavily blocked in terms of civilization, it is overbuilt, submerged. And such a source – and at the same time most open and powerful sources is the vision quest – if we do not misunderstand it as a pure procedure of self-fulfilment or what is worse a procedure of self-mirroring.

---

5   Robert Josef Kozljanič: Vision und Verantwortung. Von der Selbstverwirklichung zur Naturverwirkichung und zurück, in: Into the Wild. Innen wachsen, außen handeln. Prozessbegleitung in und mit der Natur, ed. by AGJF Sachsen, Norderstedt 2015, pp. 17–41, here 27–28

And therefore I believe that our reasoning is quite close here, albeit your position rather equals Adalbert Stifter's and mine rather this of 'Alexis Zorba' – if I am allowed to express myself metaphorically on the fly. But in my opinion both positions are fundamental in a nature-connecting life dance. A standing leg and a free leg are a prerequisite of each dance. The standing leg and the free leg can alternate with one another. When jumping high and practising similar capers an unclear or shortly suspended distribution of roles can occur. But the basic rule is: You will fall without a standing leg, without a free leg there is no sway. Both elements are equally important. And – what is interesting – among advanced dancers it is difficult to say, in individual cases, which one the standing leg and the free leg is, because the dance makes these and other rigid categories dance, sway and change – without losing rhythm!

The sense of heart and the memories of one's own childhood

Finally – but only if you can basically agree – our question could be rounded like this: Friendship with nature without an open or reopened access to crucial life sources is not possible. And: The crucial access condition is the "eye of the heart", čante ishta – as the Lakota Indians say. I shall mention here your beautiful term "sense of heart" and also when speaking of "opening the sense of heart". You wrote on February 15, 2016: "Actually I think, the sense of heart is so crucial. It opens up a new world." And just previously you gave the following example: "A child passing by hand in hand with his father shouts: 'So many pigeons!' I can feel his enthusiasm. But his father does not stop. I look up – a small flock of pigeons flies up to the roofs, I fly with them. I look into human faces like into windows: The first glance, a first resonance. You look inside and often you see chaos, tristesse, strain, and sometimes satisfaction. Some windows are complex and complicated. I experience the grief and the laughter of a child"...

Duck, geese, child, mother, grandmother

Let us linger a bit with the child and its undisguised enthusiasm about the flock of pigeons flying up. In contrast to the child the father does not stop, and by doing so he does not allow his child's enthusiasm to get close to him, or he does not notice it and walks on by pulling the child along with him ...

Here it is again, the fundamental difference, the problem: On the one hand an empathically experienced world and nature with an open heart and on the other hand passing over it with a closed heart. And at the same time, I think it shows: Childhood – one's own childhood (respectively the memories of one's own childhood) – is a source of life, too, namely a source of life that has intimately to do with the opening or closure of your own sense of heart. It is because children experience the world above all – with all advantages and drawbacks – with and through their heart. Therefore children can express unfiltered compassion, passion anger and lack of self-control. Especially the little ones can be uninhibited narcissists but equally uninhibited altruists – completely based on the gut instinct and heart level, but, if not massively disturbed from external influence, they are always dewy-eyed, in the end lovable and good-natured. The sense of heart is particularly strongly developed among children from preschool age on until adolescence (albeit often poorly refined, but mostly one-sidedly conditioned with regard to civilisation) – if it was not brutally deadened by traumatisation or abuse. This means when remembering our central childhood experience and childhood dreams we come very close to another source of life and also to the sense of heart.

As I wrote at the end of my Bettina von Arnim essay (VII. Jahrbuch für Lebensphilosophie): "Whenever we are cut off from our life sources; when we have lost the feeling for our uniquely creative aspect inside of us – for our genius; when in our inner depth suppressed and separated feelings are moving us, but cannot be articulated and do not pervade to our consciousness; when we feel to have abandoned our heart's noble path and to stray in the mists of foreign inner lands and estrangement. – Then we reflect and remember what lay before our dressage: our light-hearted childhood, the playful free, vivid child inside of us, our genius in statu nascendi. In order to achieve it, we have to climb into the magic fountain of childlike imagination: 'You won't find another way out but going back through this fountain into the magic garden of your imagination; it is not imagination, however, it is only a truth reflecting in it. The genius uses forms of imagination to impart and to awe the divine; well, you will have no other way of enjoyment in your life than the one children expect of magic caves, of deep wells; as soon as passing through them one will find blooming gardens, miracle fruit, crystal palaces where some uncomprehended music resounds [...], then you will enjoy the enthusiasm like the dancer enjoying the music.'[6]."

We adults, however, mostly act like the father in your example: We simply walk along, firmly chained within the gears of everyday life, within the work we do and our adult mind games and intellectual treadmills – running avidly the rat race of our adult pomposity and narcissism, because our hearts are hardened, our sense of heart is numbed by legal narcotics (money, work, success, power, consumerism, celerity, media, etc.). Theodor Lessing speaks in connection with these narcotics of "ecstasy surrogates" ("Rauschsurrogaten"). Genuine life ecstasies, however, according to

---

6   Bettina von Arnim: Goethes Briefwechsel mit einem Kinde, in: Werke und Briefe, vol. 2, ed. by G. Konrad, Darmstadt 1959, pp. 5–407, here p. 50

Lessing, do not numb but reconnect us with life and its life sources. How often we overlook and ignore what all children see and marvel at. We often execute and repeat instead, like under neurotic coercion, – what you described so distinctively – as our "permanent training of distancing". And we do often ignore our own inner voice of the child. We simply pass over it. And this is why these moments are so precious when we are reminded of our childhood and/or the 'child inside of us'. These moments convey a feeling of what we lose if we let our sense of heart and its world simply pass.

First attempts at
standing up

Remembering the time before dressage

We have to remember what lay prior to the civilizing conditioning and dressage. And – here Bettina von Arnim is certainly right, even if she often likes to exaggerate a bit – we need the full capacity of an undisguised, free and lively imagination. This is where we should build on and cultivate – but not civilize, train, discipline or condition! For one thing is clear: We are no longer children. It cannot be the goal at all of being or becoming child-like-only or childish-only. What I have in mind are the wild, free, playful, undisguised, light-hearted, imaginative beings we all were in our childhood: We should draw on this, and it is necessary to cherish it. This form of self-cultivation is following the guide beam of body-proximity, body-infatuation, hand in hand with the playful ego and the (good-natured) id – which is a body-pleasure-id. This is how I formulated it in my introduction to the philosophy of the body in the second yearbook for life-philosophy. I believe: such a self-cultivation fosters and develops the sense of heart. Especially when we remember all those moments when our child's heart throbbed noticeably in our chest with a feeling that was particularly warm and oceanically flowing or emanating; and also the moments when it tensed up, suffered hardship – anonymous hardship – and did not see an escape; simply all those moments when the throb of our heart was warm or hot, loving or irate, too weak or too strong, indignant or enthusiastic, anxious or longing. But above all when the throb was warm, loving, enthusiastic, passionate and longing. For in these moments we were very close to our innermost, most individual and creative centre; a creative centre that is closely related to the creative centre of the world. We are talking about moments when we feel that there are ties between our heart and the world's heart; moments when we felt how new deeper ties emerge ...

We have to draw exactly on these moments, here a powerful life source is bubbling. If we cherish this source – and do not condition or discipline but cultivate it – then we can take the sense of heart from our childhood and transfer it into our adulthood and realize it there – and 'spatialize' it.

Sense of heart + dwelling = dwelling-in-the-world (Otto Friedrich Bollnow)

The meaning of it and the effects on our existence as residents on this planet, in this landscape, in this place is demonstrated by a short glimpse at Otto Friedrich Bollnow's concept of dwelling as a loving coexistence in the inhabited space of heart-warming places. Thus we can learn that the sense of heart and living (in the sense of domiciled at heart-warming places) are correlated. In his work "Mensch und Raum"[7] Bollnow developed a dynamic notion of living in an inhabited space. This notion was the result of the charged relationship between "Expanse, distance, and the foreign" (chapter II "The wide world") concerning the emotional "security of the house" (chapter III). It finally ends in four consecutively synthesising modifications of living inside a space. 1st The space of childish and naïve emotional security. 2nd The

---

7   Otto Friedrich Bollnow: Mensch und Raum, Stuttgart 1963; English translation "Human Space", Milan 2020

state of rootlessness and homelessness (when coming of age, you are thrown out of this naïve space). 3rd The task of "reconstructing [emotional] security by building a final house". 4th The "task [...] to overcome once more the withdrawal into a fixed housing and to regain a final [emotional] security in a [comprehensive] space": this is the open space of the big wide world (in contrast to the small and narrow one); at the same time the "naïve spatiality is reconstructed on a higher level" (chapter V. "The spatiality of human life", nr. 3 "Modes of human space", p. 331).

According to Ioannis Theodoropoulos, by doing so, Bollnow denoted decisive key data of the "hermeneutics of a loving cohabitation"[8]. Echoing this spirit Theodoropoulos wrote the book "Ikiosis"[9]. His well-chosen key term is the modern Greek word *"ikiosis"* resp., ancient Greek, *oikeíosis*. *Oikeíosis*: Here the words oîkos (house, family, place of residence, native land) resound, *oikeîos* (domestic, friendly, familiar), *oikéo* (dwell, economise, live). The notion of *oikeíosis* was already in use by the Stoic. For them the meaning was: Affection, appropriation, familiarizing. I would translate it by ‚in-habitation' (in the sense of 'in-dwellization') and interpret it as 'in-habit-the-world': in order to better understand Bollnow's words "the naïve spatiality is restored on a higher level".

Cultivation of the sense of heart as the cultivation of love (Helene Stöcker)

When addressing the topic of self-cultivation then the word love or loving or devoted comes up. I do not consider it to be a coincidence. For love and the culture of love is a key element of the art of living. This is what I learned from the brilliant Nietzschean leftist Helene Stöcker – who I am intensively occupied with at the moment (I am planning the introduction and the publishing of some of her social humanistic and pacifistic works).

Stöcker originated from an Enlightenment tradition but insisted on keeping her romantic and Dionysian way of feeling and thinking. She never forgot the impulse of life she had received as a child and early juvenile: the impulse that made her heart beat so distinctly. She did not forget either what she

---

8   Ioannis E. Theodoropoulos: Otto Friedrich Bollnow – Von der Lebensphilosophie zur Hermeneutik des Lebens, in: Unser Weg 5/2009, pp. 193–200, here p. 199

9   Ioannis E. Theodoropoulos: Eine pädagogisch-anthropologische Studie der griechischen Kultur, Frankfurt a. M. 1999

owed to sciences on her path of life of authentic self-liberation and coming into the world as a free being. But as indispensable and essential sciences for Stöcker may be with regard to enlightenment, spiritual freedom and maturity: they do not have the final say. The last word has her heart. And this is why the evolvement of the heart resp. the cultivation of the sense of heart is as important as rational and critical knowledge. For how can your heart utter itself independently and in a nuanced way if it was standardized for an entire life in a bourgeois way, put in second place or even abused – instead of being treasured, loved and cultivated? We are not talking here, of course, about the sense of heart culture as it was called the education of the heart ("Herzensbildung") in the context of the bourgeois Biedermeier period. It is a matter of cultivation of the heart of free individuals, the culture of the heart of "revolutionary man"[10]. In this case the cultivation of love plays a key role as well as the cultivation of righteous wrath – a wrath that enrages and helpingly revolts when crude injustice happens to the weak. A third key role can be ascribed to the ability of breaking ranks or going against the tide – exactly during those moments when your own voice of the heart of love or wrath indicate it – ethically – advisable. So it happened that Stöcker followed her voice of the heart during the outbreak of World War I and uncompromisingly assumed the pacifist position. The war fever and warmongering of most Germans was repulsive and alien to her. In her diary entries dated October 15, 1914, we read: "These are not only insanities of the brain but also of the heart, so we can speak of a moral insanity."[11] And on November 21, 1914 she writes: „Where lies the crudeness of humans: In the stupidity of the head or the narrowness of the heart? I almost think, it is in the head. They are not as evil as they are thoughtless, undiscriminating, and suggestible. You can make them believe everything. If you tell them that murdering people is good, 'good for something', they simply believe it, – and even more so, they do it with a clear conscience 'for their fatherland'. Ethical illiterates" (ibid. p. 160).

Here we can see that another crucial competence must be added to the development of the sense of heart: the proper incorruptible critical faculty, the impartiality of the proper judgment – a free head as the culmination of a body fond of life with a good-natured and strong heart.

10   On the concept of „revolutionary man" cf: Helene Stöcker: Zur Einführung, in: Karoline Michaelis: Eine Auswahl ihrer Briefe, ed. by H. Stöcker, Berlin 1912, pp. V–XXVIII, here p. XV
11   Helene Stöcker: Vor zehn Jahren! in: Die Neue Generation, 7-8/1924, pp. 145–161, here p. 157

Although Stöcker believed that the demands of the heart and those of reason have the same source and direction, she was unsettled and a little disillusioned at this point in her life. Almost in despair about her ideals and deeply depressed, she wrote after the outbreak of World War I in 1914: "If we could not hope that human love and goodness become reality some time, then we don't want to live such a life. This is the meaning of life, at least for me" (ibid. p. 155). And more aggravated in 1939: "The breakdown of our European culture unfolding anew through this murderous war has hit me hard. I had to set aside my hopes for a harmonious creation of human relations to a very modest scale. But as insecure and uncertain our hopes for the fulfilment of our ideals for a higher humanity and a happy human existence may be – I am still full of an irrational love for life and for humans – however many disappointments life and humans may have brought. –"[12]. Here we can see as well: In the critical moment she follows the voice of her heart – that "irrational love for life and for humans"; even if this may not be reasonable (in the sense of 'realistic').

Thus Stöcker always remained faithful to her principle of a new free culture of love. On the occasion of the new edition of her novel "Liebe"[13] in 1924 Helene Stöcker clearly and concisely summarized the basic intention of her literary major work. This summary is so revealing, because it is a programme and equally a manifesto of Helene Stöcker's entire life philosophy – her so-called "new ethics" ("Neue Ethik").

"This book [...] has a goal to which all our work is dedicated: an enhancement and reinforcement of our personal culture of love. It wants to illustrate the tragedy of a mentally-sensuous passion which man and woman experience in many phases of their development but – despite their ardent endeavour – they cannot completely reach one another; the eternal misunderstanding of two humans, one of them wants to change the world, the other one just wants to watch and understand it.

This book is also a trial – and maybe new in its kind – to express uncompromisingly the emotional experience of a woman's love – in the mutual conditionality of the mental and physical state – and the almost irresolvable dilemma in the love of a human being, who is both woman

---

12   From a curriculum vitae written by Helene Stöcker in 1939. Published in: Ariadne
      – Almanach des Archivs der deutschen Frauenbewegung, 5/1986
13   Helene Stöcker: Liebe, existing in several editions – First edition Berlin 1922

and personality at the same time. It finally aims – and perhaps above all – at bridging the chasms between humans based on the tragic recognition of the 'irresponsibility of man for his being and his existence' to reach that ethical tolerance; it wants to achieve that supreme form of justice towards human imperfection which means 'love with one's eyes open'! In the firm conviction that despite all present economic and political distress, the struggle for a more soulful form of sexual love constitutes a necessary task in the eternal human strive for higher forms of existence. May these new volumes also – as documents of such a struggle – go out again and get into the hands of those, who together with me, despite the darkness of the present, believe in the human race, no – even more in humanity."[14]

The summary mentions five main goals:

1) Enhancement of the personal culture of love towards a more affectionate and just mutual realization and appreciation (spiritually mental self-cultivation of love).

2) Enhancement of the personal culture of love towards a mentally sensuous passion and sexuality (physically mental self-cultivation of love).

3) Deliberate permission and integration of the follow tragic dissent and polarities: male-female, egocentric-sentiocentric, physical-psychological, libidinal-personal, ... (dealing with or enduring existential dissent, acting out dramatically and productively).

4) Unreserved permission of addressing female experience of love and love life (liberation and cultivation of female-erotic selfhood)

5) The attempt requiring patience, trust, and a spirit of conciliation despite the irresponsibility and shortcomings of humans and to help – together with them! – shape a more human future (belief in humanity preferably without any illusion).

---

14 Helene Stöcker: [Announcement of the new edition of her book] Liebe, in: Die Neue Generation 12/1924, p. 317

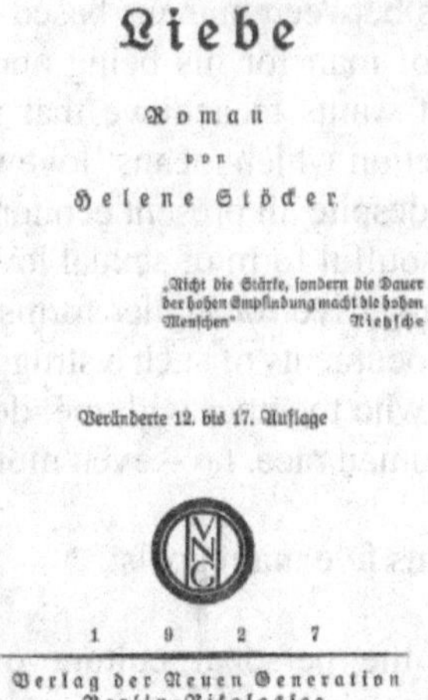

Book cover: "Love". A novel by Helene Stöcker

Sense of heart cultivation in childhood. The fictional story of Little Tree

That's more or less how I would imagine sense of heart cultivation within the framework of a life-philosophical tradition. An impression of an deeply human cultivating concept of the sense of heart can be found in the (children's book and) book for young people by Forrest Carter "The Education of Little Tree"[15].

„The Education of Little Tree" is a book that fascinated and influenced me in my youth and still fascinates me today. And for this reason that so many things we have been talking about are dealt with at a very humane level – in the absence of hierarchy and priestcraft.

The fictional story of Little Tree takes place some time after the displacement of the Cherokee from their ancestral lands. This displacement went down in history under the name "Trail of Tears" and happened in the winter of 1838/39. During this trail half of the 13,000 displaced Cherokee had lost their life under the worst and most brutal circumstances.

---

15   Forrest Carter: The Education of Little Tree, first edition New York 1976

After this (quasi 'Stalinistic') displacement the Cherokee nation was fragmented, culturally half broken and 'civilized'. (Annotation made by Forrest Carter to the "Trail of Tears": „And so they called it Trail of Tears. Not because the Cherokee cried; for he did not. They called it the Trail of Tears for it sounds romantic and speaks of the sorrow of those who stood by the Trail. A death march is not romantic."[16] Not all of the Cherokee were driven together and displaced by the soldiers. Few of them fled into the faraway woods and mountains and were thus able to avoid their displacement; among them – according to the fictional story – the Little Tree's family (cf. pp. 42–43).

Little Tree's grandfather was half Cherokee and his grandmother was full Cherokee. They lived alone in the mountains of Tennessee, hundreds of kilometres in the East away from the new homeland of the displaced Cherokee Indians. In any case, the tribal union was more or less destroyed. The time of the old indigenous, free, pre-civilized Indian life of the Cherokee tribe was over. Forced by the white man, the situation which the Cherokee and so many other indigenous peoples then (and today) had to endure, is remotely similar to ours, because we, respectively our Celtic and Germanic ancestors, had to go through roughly 2000 years of military conquest, forced civilization and forced Christianisation – all this in several successions, of course, (the Roman conquest of Rhaetia, forced edicts of Theodosius, several waves of evangelisation, and the witch-hunt later then ...) But these heart deafening and internally devastating traumatisations – which are at the beginning of all forced civilizations – date back such along time run over longer intervals thus offering quite different possibilities of adaptation and integration.

Well, this comparison may be far-fetched. Anyway one thing is clear: Our fictional 'hero' Little Tree, his early deceased parents and his grandparents had found themselves catapulted into the modern US civilization. A return to the autonomous, indigenous community life was no longer possible for them. They already experienced at first hand the effect of alienation from nature and the suppression of the sense of heart brought by the white civilization – and nevertheless they tried to live in close touch with nature, tried to further their sense of heart and to follow its signals. And this makes their situation quite comparable to ours.

In this story the sense of heart is stronger in the limelight than in other stories I know. Moreover: Forrest Carter's childhood fiction is a story of

---

16   Forrest Carter: The Education of Little Tree, Albuquerque 1986, p. 42

educating the sense of heart of a fictional Cherokee boy, whose parents had died in the woods, where he had to grow up with his grandparents – in the neighbourhood of white farmers, merchants, and villagers.

Here the development of the capacity to love and the capacity of loving understanding is central, too. Little Tree's Indian grandmother tells him about the two souls that exist in their culture: the "body soul" and the "spirit soul". (Here the potentially sounding body-soul dualism should not be taken too seriously. Indigenous-mythical cultures do not know such a dualism as a rule, because body and soul are inseparably entangled in an animistic and panpsychistic worldview: the example of the "tree soul" is eye-opening ...) The "spirit soul" comes really close to what we understood by the sense of heart.

"Granma said everybody has two minds. One of the minds has to do the necessaries for the body living. You had to use it to figure how to get shelter and eating and such like for the body. She said you had to use it to mate and have young'uns and such. She said we had to have that mind so as we could carry on. But she said we had another mind that had nothing atall to do with such. She said it was the spirit mind. Granma said if you used the body-living mind to think greedy or mean; if you was always cuttin' at folks with it and figuring how to material profit off'n them ... then you would shrink up your spirit mind to a size no bigger'n a hickor'nut. Granma said that when your body died, the body-living mind died with it, and if that's the way you had thought all your life there you was, stuck with a hickor'nut spirit, as the spirit mind was all that lived when everything else died. [...] That's how you become dead people. Granma said you could easy spot dead people; [...] when they looked at a tree they saw nothing but lumber and profit; never beauty. Granma said they was dead people walking around. Granma said that the spirit mind was like any other muscle. If you used it it got bigger and stronger. She said the only way it could get that way was using it to understand, but you couldn't open the door to it until you quit being greedy and such with your body mind. Then understanding commenced to take up, and the more you tried to understand, the bigger it got. Natural, she said, understanding and love was the same thing [...]. I see right out that I was going to commence trying to understand practical everybody, for I sure didn't want to come up with a hickor'nut spirit."[17]

---

17   Ibid., pp. 59–60; on the subject of understanding and loving cf. also the story of Coon Jack, pp. 38–39

The sense of heart and the personal "secret place"

For the development of the "spirit mind" resp. of the sense of heart a "secret place" is necessary: a favourite place, a truly personal heartfelt place in Mother Nature. Every Cherokee, according to the fictional story, has his "secret place", that is what the Cherokee grandmother told her grandson. "She said she reckined most everybody had a secret place, but she couldn't be certain, as she had never made inquiries of it. Granma said it was necessary. Which made me feel quite good about having one." (p. 59). The "secret place" in Mother Nature is a vital learning environment: „Granma said I could watch some of how it worked from my secret place. In the spring when everything is born (and always, when anything is born, even an idea), there's fret and fuss. There's spring storms like a baby borning in blood and pain. Granma said it was the spirits kicking up a fuss at having to get back into material forms again. Then there was the summer – our growed-up lives – and autumn when we got older and had that peculiar feeling in our spirits of being back in time.

Some folks called it nostalgia and sadness. The winter with everything dead or seeming to be, like our bodies when they die, but born again just like the spring. Granma said the Cherokees knew, and had learned it long ago." (pp. 60-61). And a "secret place" is not only necessary to get to know good knowledge about the life cycle, but much more specifically, to experience heart attachment to the place, to understand individual animals and plants, to receive heartfelt knowledge about other animated beings. "Granma said I would come to know that the old sweet gum tree in my secret place had a spirit too. Not a spirit of humans, but a tree spirit. She said her Pa had taught her all about it. Granma's Pa was called Brown Hawk. She said his understanding was deep. He could feel the tree-thought." (p. 61)

Childlike distress, communication with nature and consolation

Sometimes when I read in this book full of wisdom of the heart, I have a lump in my throat at the particularly intensive passages. Everybody knows this lump. Then I also realise what I repress in everyday life: how heartless our adult life mostly is, you know; and – in the words of Lewis Mumford and Fabian Scheidler – how deeply engaged we are in this heart-devouring "megamachine" called civilization. There is no way out.

I do not weep too often. I can be quite tough, too if necessary. But in such 'Little Tree moments' I would like to cry – and do so sometimes. And then I feel this cathartic effect, feel my sense of heart opening, my heart beating stronger, and old memories arouse, how I get access to the source of my own childlike imagination and heartfelt world experience. Let me give you just one example of a passage at the end of the book. As mentioned before Little Tree came to his grandparents at the age of five. When he was six, he was taken away from them by court decision and put into a far away Christian orphanage lead by a priest. Miraculously shortly afterwards, he came back to his grandparents, stayed with them until they died. Then, at the age of 10/11 he struggled along with his two dogs as a harvest hand westbound to the new 'homeland' of the Cherokee.

But at the age of six he had this bitter experience in the orphanage, far away from home as the only Indian boy being discriminated against. One scene from a lesson: The schoolmistress "held up a picture that showed a deer herd coming out of a spring branch. They was jumping on one another and it looked like they was pushing to get out of the water." (p. 190) The mistress asks whether the pupils knew what the deer were doing. Some say, the deer are probably trying to escape the hunter. Others think they are afraid of the water. Little Tree puts up his hand and says: "I seen right off they was mating; for it was buck deer that was jumping the does; also, I could tell by the bushes and trees that it was the time of the year when they done their mating." (p. 190) The schoolmistress is flabbergasted. She shouts: "I should have *known* – we *all* should have known … filth … filth … would come out of you … you … little *bastard*." (p. 191) She takes him to the priest, and he scolds: "You are born of evil, so I know repentance is not in you; but praise God, you are going to be taught not to inflict your evil upon Christians. You can't repent … but you shall cry out!" (p. 191) With these words the priest brutally whips him with a stick until blood runs down his naked back and legs into the shoes. Banished from lessons and the evening meal, Little Tree later stands by the window in the dormitory. After sunset he looks up to the Dog Star (Sirius). As his grandmother taught him, he communicates via the star with his grandparents and with Willow John, an old Indian friend of the family. "I told them I had no way in the world of knowing how I made the lady sick; nor what come over the Reverend. […] I told Granpa that it 'peared to me that more than likely I couldn't hardly no way atall handle the situation. I said I wanted to come home. […] Every evening after that, when dusk brought the Dog Star up, I told Granma and Granpa and Willow John I wanted to come home. I would not see the pictures they sent, nor listen. [...] Three nights later, the Dog Star was hid by heavy clouds. Wind tore down a light pole and the orphanage was dark. I knew they had heard. [...] Outside now, I spent all my time under the oak tree. She was supposed to be asleep, but she said she wasn't, on account of me. She talked slow – and low. Late one evening, just before we was to go in, I thought I seen Granpa. It was a tall man and he wore a big black hat. He was moving away from me down the street. I run to the iron fence and hollered, 'Granpa! Granpa!' He didn't turn." (p. 192-193) Later it turned out that the man with the hat was Willow John. He had met the grandparents beforehand. For all three of them were very worried about Little Tree – each time they looked up to the Dog Star. Immediately afterwards Willow John had started his long journey to the orphanage without telling the others. Then he had pursued the priest for two days. Finally he stood in his office and "said that Little Tree was to come home to the mountains." Thereupon the priest, who did not want to do anything with this "savage", signed the release papers (p. 204). Shortly afterwards Little Tree was taken back to the mountains by his grandfather. The following Sunday they meet Willow John, this old doleful Indian living half a day's march away from the village.

Forrest Carter told about him beforehand: "The eyes were black, open wounds; not angry wounds, but dead wounds that lay bare, without life. You couldn't tell if the eyes were dim, or if Willow John was looking past you into a dimness far away. Once, in later years, an Apache showed me a picture of an old man. It was Go-khla-yeh, Geronimo. He had the eyes of Willow John. Willow John was over eighty. Grandpa said that long ago, Willow John had gone to the nations. He had walked the mountains, and would not ride in a car or train. He was gone three years and came back; but he would not talk of it. He would only say there was no nation." (p. 147) And now Little Tree sees Willow John again for the first time after his stay in the orphanage. "Willow John was standing back in the trees, where I knew he would be; the old straight-brimmed black hat settin' on top of his head. I run as hard as I could and grabbed Willow John around the legs and hugged him. I said, Thankee, Willow John.' He didn't say anything but reached and touched my shoulder. When I looked up, his eyes was twinkling and shining, black deep." (p. 205)

Little Tree does not only go to see Willow John as soon as possible but he also goes to his "secret place". "I come back slow down the trail and found my secret place. It was just like the picture Granma had sent me [via

Dog-Star-communication]. [...] The pines whispered and the wind picked up, and they commenced to sing, 'Little Tree is home ... Little Tree is home! Listen to our song! Little Tree is with us. Little Tree is home!' They hummed it low and sung it higher, and the spring branch sung it too along with them. The hounds noticed, for they quit sniffing the ground and stood with their ears up and listened. The hounds knew and come around me and laid down, content with the feeling. Through that short winter day, I lay in my secret place. And my spirit didn't hurt anymore. I was washed clean by the feeling song of the wind and the trees and the spring branch and the birds." (p. 203)

Anguish of heart, deep recall and healing

So far the passage including the context: Why am I reproducing this passage so explicitly? Why these long quotations? Why this story of a child's great distress along with a happy turnaround? This is because I am of the opinion that there is something to this fictional story (and similar stories), some salutary effect, something that opens the sense of heart, something that makes our heart beat in a certain way, something that brings back memories. And I think that this cannot be (easily) achieved otherwise: Moments of a deeply moved pause and appreciation. And through this pause and appreciation I can remember similar moments. Moments I lived through as a child, moments of despair of the heartless world of adults with their hostile laws towards nature, pleasure, human body, and civilizing constraints. Key moments to which I was 'initiated' in this civilized world as a child and adolescent: by forced and painful self-schism. In order to survive I had to learn how to divide belly, head, and heart (the 'best' way to become a well-adapted civilization psychotic); I had to learn how to treat my naïve feeling of justice, under the pressure of social conventions, as something leprous to be put in quarantine (the 'best' way, to choke a sound feeling of responsibility); I had to learn to discipline myself, i.e. sitting quietly for hours and monotonously learn and work in an alienated way (to put in quarantine the most vivid thing I had and have, which is my body) – all this only to fulfil my duty of compulsory schooling, military service resp. civilian service, work and other duties (the 'best' way to become an inwardly dead person already during one's lifetime, a civilization zombie); I had to learn to classify my own perceptions, experiencing, judgements as 'untrue' and 'unreal' under the pressure of social and publicly, nationally, governmentally regulated 'truths' and 'realities' (the 'best' way to choke all feelings of truth and reality); I had to learn that my most sacred feelings, my most yearning desires, my most tender thoughts have no place in this world. Always had I to civilize, to discipline, to reprimand, to condition myself. In this process of civilization, it is also a matter of exterminating all possible naiveté and thus all nativity. For naiveté and nativity are closely connected. (How did Forrest Carter put it? "Me and Granpa thought Indian. Later people would tell me that this is naive – but I knew – and I remembered what Granpa said about 'words'. If it is 'naive', it does not matter, for it is also good. Granpa said it would always carry me through … which it has" (p. 123).)

Anyway there was no talk of a culture of love, of the cultivation of those things that lay close to my heart and to the heart of others. What is meant by the bourgeois german word "Herzensbildung" (education of the heart) mostly is a harmless affair where the 'radical capacity for love', 'righteous anger' and 'independent judgement' are mitigated. Even the established Christian churches – having in the Sermon on the Mount a promising (and developable) example of a great culture of love – have failed here. For when they had to get down to the nitty-gritty (e.g. their power of definition) the answer to everything was that clerical duties and commandments were more important than the promptings of the heart. Fortunately, however, there was not only this world that is foreign and estranged to the heart. There was another world, too: the world of friends/girlfriends, of nature and the promptings of my heart. And there were recorded stories from this different world. If these stories had not existed; more than that: if these loving friends/girlfriends had not existed, if the quiet spots of untouched nature had not existed, my tender and innermost heart would not have powerfully revolted so many times, and if I had not listened to my heart, to nature and my friends and had not followed it, albeit it often was so hard and depressing to swim against the tide; who knows what would have become of me, maybe a miserable and pathetic individual, a civilization zombie like Dieter Bohlen? (Singer/musician and one of the judges in the German TV show: "Deutschland sucht den Superstar" or "Germany's got talent"). A priest who indulges in the dark what he is not allowed to do in public light? A businessman who perfectly masters to cheat others to make a big haul? A diplomatic power politician who, pale faced and woolly, talks a lot but says as little as possible? A power-obsessed and money-grubbing corporation manager to whom positions and bonus payments are more important than the life of thousands and thousands of people and creatures he severely disturbs or even completely destroys?

Mustering all one's courage at last

There is the trick: All these civilizing divisions have to be constantly artificially maintained. In this context you used this nice metaphor in your last writing: The beach is under the pavement, yes that's true. And even in such a rationalized, mechanized world of medialisation deep and fierce gut instincts, warm and loving heartfelt feelings, feelings of wrath claiming justice, and not appropriated thoughts and judgements can be noticed. Every spring at innumerable places small grass plants blow up the tarmac. Now as before uncounted sunrises, filled with sacred feelings, glow at the horizon.

And deep inside of us they are all present: the memories of what lay before the conditioning and dressage. This is why books like those by Forrest Carter are so important: They bring these important memories back. When reading "The Education of Little Tree" I can live through (share, relive) how the world responded and helped me (whatever the appearance and case) in the hour of my abysmal, heartfelt distress, entirely on the level of my heart – be it in the case of a beloved person, be it in the case of a star in the sky, be it in the case of a beloved place, tree or animal to which I talked and confided my heart's distress. During these and similar heartfelt moments of distress, I think, we experience a liberation of the heart and an opening of the sense of heart. Here the sense of the basic trust is regained and/or deepened. But then we have to venture out ourselves – and by 'we' and 'ourselves' I mean the (adult and 'overgrown') civilized individuals – of the casing and gearbox of our civilized world. We have to circumvent in an act of rebellion all the internal civilizing barriers and divisions with a dance-like life. We have to take our heart in our own hands and venture the first step. This can be hard, really hard. But if we have the consent of the good-natured heart of our living body and its pleasures, then it is not hard at all. Montaigne put it in a splendid way: "I, who always remain attached to the earth, am repelled by that misanthropic wisdom which wants to make physical culture contemptible and hateful to us. I find it equally absurd to dislike the natural pleasures of the heart as to make it too attached to them. ... One should neither run after the lusts nor run away from them – one should welcome them. I even welcome them with somewhat more ready and wider arms than usual, for I follow more easily my natural inclination."

„I got a feeling"

Well, but the first steps and the awakening is an art in itself. You suggested, with your life experience and subtlety, the importance of 'circle-enabling' steps as the first steps and not circle-breaking awakenings, i.e. steps like in a circle dance – but with the possibility of getting out of line. We are talking about rebellion, but not a rebellion which breaks up, breaks to pieces, and destroys but one that rounds, rounds off, rounds anew ... And together with this rebellion, which can and shall open up nature-friendly and human-friendly future places, forces leading to sources of life are called for, scoops from the wells of child memories and a skilful and patient cultivation of the sense of heart.

Hoping that my attempt of a rounding was not a lonely but a mutual one,

I remain with sense of heart felt regards

R. J. K.

6.
Interim Remarks. Addendum from the Years 2023–2024

When I (R. J. Kozljanič) wrote this email in 2017, the only thing I knew about Forrest Carter (1925-1979) was what I read on page two of my edition of the book "Der Stern der Cherokee"[1]: "Forrest Carter, born in 1925, was taken in by his Native American grandparents as an orphan at the age of five. They familiarised him with the traditions of the Cherokee. When his grandparents also died prematurely, he travelled all over the country, sometimes earning money as a cowboy. He acquired his knowledge of Native American history himself."

Six years later, in 2023, when I was busy revising the English-language edition of this letter dialogue, I found out that Forrest Carter was distantly related to the Cherokee, but the story about Little Tree was not autobiographical but invented, at least over extended passages. And that's not all: Forrest Carter was actually called Asa Earl Carter. He lived in the southern states of the USA from 1925 until his death in 1979 and agitated in the 1950s and 1960s as a "white supremacist", and an uncompromising US fascist. He wrote and held racist and anti-Semitic speeches and radio programmes, founded a violent Ku Klux Klan local group, operated and supported racist segregation policies and propaganda in a variety of ways. In 1970, he wanted to become governor of Alabama with his own fascist election programme. He failed, withdrew from politics and became a writer[2].

Although Forrest Carter later denied the identity with Asa Earl Carter, this identity was posthumously confirmed by his divorced wife. This was

---

1   "The Star of the Cherokee" = German title of "The Education of Little Tree", Forrest Carter: Der Stern der Cherokee, dtv edition München 1982

2   See Wikipedia: https://en.wikipedia.org/wiki/Asa_Earl_Carter – accessed August 31, 2023

shortly after "The Education of Little Tree" had won the ABBY Award (American Booksellers Book of the Year). This meant that by the end of 1991 at the latest, twelve years after his death, it was clear that Forrest and Asa Earl Carter were the same person. Nevertheless, it took (and still takes) time for this truth, which is irritating for all Little Tree fans, to reach the general public.

"The Education of Little Tree" was made into a film by Paramount Pictures Hollywood, in 1997. The director and (co-)writer was Richard Friedenberg. His assessment of the 'Carter case' was as follows: "Here was this guy, who did bad things, disappeared off the face of the earth in Alabama, where he was a Ku Kluxer, and reappeared in the Oklahoma-Texas area near the Cherokee reservation of the western Cherokee nation, where he proceeded to write several books. It strikes me, he spent his literary life, and whoever he was in his second phase, in some kind of grand apology for his first life."[3] There is much to be said in favour of this explanation. In the following, I will show why I also broadly agree with this explanation.

When I learnt about Carter's past political machinations, my first reaction was shock, frustration and outrage. I wanted to delete the whole Little Tree passage from the letter dialogue as quickly as possible. And then know nothing more about it. The second reaction was to gather more information about the case and then let it sink in. Finally, I picked up the book again and read it from a completely new perspective. My guiding questions were: Are there racist or anti-Semitic insinuations and suggestions in the book - obvious or hidden? Is the story of Little Tree in any way influenced by the anti-humanist and fascist ideas of Asa Earl Carter from the 50s and 60s? My answer: No. Everything that Carter stood up for and fought for in his earlier days comes off badly in "Little Tree". It is as if Carter has 'gone from Saul to Paul' with this book. I would like to illustrate this with a few examples.

First the white politician: When Little Tree and his grandfather are back in the village, a politician comes by and gives election speeches. He strongly resembles the types of politicians Carter used to write speeches for (such as

---

3   Quoted in: Weinraub, Bernard: Movie With a Murky Background: The Man Who Wrote the Book, The New York Times, December 17, 1997. See: https://en.wikipedia.org/wiki/The_Education_of_Little_Tree_(film) – accessed August 31, 2023

the segregationist George Wallace); and arguably resembles the character Carter himself used to be. From the outset, the politician is portrayed as a calculating, hypocritical and loud-mouthed phoney. This politician also uses very similar scapegoating and hate rhetoric as Carter did in his time, except that instead of blacks and Jews, Catholics are targeted. On arriving in the village, the politician shakes hands with everyone except Grandpa and Little Tree. "Granpa said this was because we looked like Indians and didn't vote nohow, so we was of practical no use whatsoever to the politician"[4].

"He wore a black coat and had a white shirt with a ribbon tied at his neck; it was black and hung down. He laughed a lot and 'peared to be mighty happy. That is, until he got mad. He got up on a box and commenced to get worked up about conditions in Washington City … which he said was total going to hell. He said it wasn't a thing in the world but Sodom and Gomorrah, which I guess it was. He got madder and madder about it and untied the ribbon around his neck. He said the Catholics was behind every damn bit of it. He said they was practical in control of the whole thing, and was aiming to put Mr. Pope in the White House. Catholics, he said, was the rottenest, low-downest snakes that ever lived" etc. p. p. (p. 82).

Grandpa later comments on this speech: "iff'n ye taken a knife and cut fer half a day into that politician's gizzard, ye'd have a hard time finding a kernel of truth." The politician was not interested in the real problems and needs of ordinary people: "Ye'll notice the son of a bitch didn't say a thing" about real life (p. 85).

And to Little Tree's question "do ye know any Catholics?" Grandpa answers: "I seen one oncet […] didn't look particular mean … though I figgered he had been in some kind of scrape … he had got his collar twisted up, and more than likely was jest drunk enough that he failed to notice it. He 'peared to be, howsoever, peaceful enough." (p. 85). „Granpa said that wasn't no doubt in his mind that the Catholics would like to git control … but he said iff'n ye had a hog and ye didn't want it stole, jest git ten or twelve men to guard it, each one of which wanted to steal it. He said that hog would be safe as in yer own kitchen. Granpa said they was all so crooked in Washington City, that they had to watch one another all the

---

4   Forrest Carter: The Education of Little Tree, Albuquerque 1986, pp. 81-82 – Originally published New York 1976

time. Granpa said that they was so many trying to git control, it was a continual dogfight all the time anyhow. He said the worst thing wrong with Washington City was it had so many damn politicians in it" (p. 86).

Shortly afterwards it was said that rich businessmen and company bosses in Washington were playing politics against ordinary people: "they was trying hard as they could, bribing politicians practical every day in Washington City." (p. 86)

White politicians and powerful businessmen therefore come off very badly. They are consistently portrayed as false, calculating, deceitful and highly untrustworthy. Their thinking and behaviour is almost always corrupt, greedy and inhumane. Above all, they are interested in power and money. The following applies to such businessmen and politicians: The big-heads never take risks, at least not when it comes to their money.

Carter obviously knew what he was talking about. It was a similar story with the white "Christian" man who offered Little Tree a "Christian trade" and cheated him by selling him a sick calf that died shortly afterwards (p. 83f and 86f). Grandpa commented on this: "Ye see, Little Tree, ain't no way of learning, except by letting ye do. Iff'n I had stopped ye from buying the calf, ye'd have always thought ye'd ought to had it. Iff'n I'd told ye to buy it, ye'd blame me fer the calf dying. Ye'll have to learn as ye go" (p. 87).

The lesson is clear: do not trust any politician, businessman or churchman – not even a senior teacher or expert; do not trust any of the powerful; do not trust those who have been taken into service by the powerful. But: trust your own senses, your own life experiences, trust those who are really good for you without ulterior motives. And in this sense: make your own experiences and become wise, become life-wise.

The world of white high civilisation is a false, wrong, greedy and violent world. Its spokespeople and authorities are basically not to be trusted. This applies not only to politicians and businessmen, but also to the education system, priests and state teachers, policemen and soldiers, academics and newspaper writers.

In principle, only the ordinary, down-to-earth, non-philistine people who tend to be poor come off well – and those who help them, who show solidarity with them ideally and/or materially. Above all, they are the ones who have their hearts in the right place. But they – Indians, small farmers, ordinary citizens and craftsmen, self-sufficient people and their sympathisers – are also the ones who are ignored, marginalised, oppressed, traumatised, exploited or even murdered by the ruling white class and its profiteers and followers. The ordinary and solidary people do not belong to any kind of 'elite', no institution of power, no party or established ideology. They are not or hardly corrupted by high civilisation and live in solidarity in and from their basic culture.

"Grandpa had all the natural enemies of a mountain man. Add on to that he was poor without saying and more Indian than not. I suppose today, the enemies would be called 'the establishment,' but to Granpa, whether sheriff, state or federal revenue agent, or politician of any stripe, he called them 'the law', meaning powerful monsters who had no regard for how folks had to live and get by" (p. 16). – But not all whites were hostile and greedy, for example, the family of Grandpa's Pa – Scottish immigrants. They "were mountain bred. They did not lust for land, or profit, but loved freedom of the mountains, as did the Cherokee" (p. 43).

And they understand and accept the first great basic rule that runs through the human and natural world: it is about balanced and equalising give and take and, when in doubt, about giving more than you take. Just like Grandpa taught Little Tree: "It is The Way [...]. Take only what ye need. When ye take the deer, do not take the best. Take the smaller and the slower and then the deer will grow stronger and always give meat. Pa-koh, the panther, knows and so must ye. [...] Only Ti-bi, the bee, stores more than he can use ... and so he is robbed by the bear, and the 'coon ... and the Cherokee. It is so with people who store and fat themselves with more than their share. They will have it taken from them. And there will be wars over it ... and they will make long talks, trying to hold more than their share. They will say a flag stands for their right to do this ... and men will die because of the words and the flag ... but they will not change the rules of The Way" (pp. 9-10).

In addition to this rule, there is a second great basic rule: understanding and forgiveness, or more precisely: understanding and loving. These two are connected and they belong together indeed. Understanding is more important than (pre-)judgement. This is illustrated by the story of Coon Jack – the keeper of the keys to the church cupboard with the hymn books.

This story took place in Grandpa's youth. As a young lad, Grandpa made fun of Coon Jack because he made himself so important. Grandpa said "… his Pa told him, 'Son, don't laugh at 'Coon Jack. Ye see, when the Cherokee was forced to give up his home and go to the Nations, 'Coon Jack was young, and he hid out in these mountains, and he fought to hold on. When the War 'tween the States come, he saw maybe he could fight the same guvmin, and get back the land and homes. He fought hard. Both times he lost. When the War ended, the politicians set in, trying to git what was left of what we had. 'Coon Jack fought, and run, and hid, and fought some more. Ye see, 'Coon Jack come up in the time of fighting. All he's got now is the key to the songbook box. And if 'Coon Jack seems to be cantankerous … well, there ain't nothing left for 'Coon Jack to fight. He never knowed nothing else.' Granpa said, he come might near crying fer 'Coon Jack. He said after that, it didn't matter what 'Coon Jack said, or did … he loved him, because he understood him. Granpa said that such was 'kin,' and most of people's mortal trouble come about by not practicing it; from that and the politicians" (p. 39).

There is a third basic rule. It always resonates, but is not made explicit anywhere in the text. I put it in the following words: Believe in the good in people and do good yourself – but don't let the elitists and money egoists (vulgo: "sons of bitches" cf. p. 85) and their high civilisation blind you and take the piss.

As the story with 'Coon Jack and other passages (cf. pp. 44-45) suggest, the Southern US-States come off somewhat better than the Northern US-States. This could conceal a residual segregationist bias, a residual racist resentment on Carter's part. Let's take a closer look. As we know, the US 'Civil' War was not only about the independence of the individual states but also about the issue of slavery. The ruling elite of the Southern US-States – a small but powerful group of land-owning, slave-holding oligarchs – wanted to hold on to slavery as their 'business model', while the Northern US-States did not. Does Carter take sides with them? No, he does not, because ultimately there is no doubt here either: this Southern elite is also part of the "establishment", they too and their policies are no better than the government in Washington. They too use and exploit ordinary people, which is why 'Coon Jack's hope was illusory from the start that the Cherokee would get their land back. Here Carter leaves no doubt about it. That is so far as the Indians are concerned.

But what about black people here? Do black people appear in the story of Little Tree? As far as I can see, only in one passage, in the chapter "The Farm in the Clearing" (pp. 114-122). In addition to the one-legged war invalid and his wife (along with two small, hungry daughters), there is an old and frail black man ("old black man"). After the Civil War, all five of them settled on a lonely and run-down farm without any means, without livestock or seed, neither money nor food. They are fighting for survival. In their desperation, they pull the plough themselves, the woman and her one-legged man with a prosthesis in front. The black man steers and operates the plough as best he can. A sergeant from the North sees this by chance and takes pity on these poor Southern farmers. He gives them a mule and corn seed. Together with a young private from his company, he helps them in his spare time. The sergeant and his private plough, till and plant apple trees. This is how the southerners slowly get back on their feet. In this entire chapter not a single word or suggestion is made about the black old man that is negative, quite the opposite. Supported by mutual recognition and human solidarity, everyone lives with and for each other, helping and rejoicing together that things are looking up again. The fact that the story ends badly after all is only, because the poor farmers are eventually evicted by the bailiff's "sheriffs". (A rich white man eventually snatches up the farm.) The old black man and the invalid white man put up a desperate and brave defence. They are shot. So is the northern sergeant. The wife and children are driven away. It later became known that the young private had deserted. "He was posted as a coward, running out on an uprising and all" (p. 122).

So far as this passage is concerned, I see a lot of humanity and solidarity, mutual respect and desperate self-defence in it, as well as a certain criticism of blind military obedience to orders and the "establishment" of the power elites – but certainly no white supremacy racism and no glorification of the South. Here, too, my assessment is similar to Friedenberg's, who noted that the few Blacks and Jews in Carter's books are portrayed in a consistently sympathetic manner. "The bad guys are almost, without fail, rich whites, politicians and phony preachers."[5]

---

5   Quoted in: Weinraub, Bernard: Movie With a Murky Background: The Man Who Wrote the Book, The New York Times, December 17, 1997. See: https:// en.wikipedia.org/wiki/The_Education_of_Little_Tree_(film) – accessed August 31, 2023

For all these reasons, I also tend to agree with the overall assessment of Richard Friedenberg, who was so fascinated by the book because "characters and milieu they were in represented everything that was good about America and everything that was bad."[6]

I would just express it in a less US-narcissistic way. And say: the book is carried and flooded with a warm and simple humanity, it joins the multitude of Rousseauist texts and theses that more or less all proclaim that man is, as Rutger Bregman recently put it, "basically good"[7]. And is only corrupted and deformed by processes and institutions of power civilisation, by power propaganda, ideological prejudice and resentments.

Carter may have been a vile fascist and misanthrope in his political days. Obviously, he later turned from Saul to Paul as a writer. His book may be pure (or almost pure) fiction. Some crucial things remain. For example that this book was and is a deeply human and nature-connecting liberation text for many people. Or that it calls for faith in the good in people and in nature. Or that it strengthens self-awareness and self-authorisation as well as the experience of nature and the understanding of others ("to understand is to love"). We can learn what this might be not from the eccentric Nietzsche, but from Forrest Carter's down-to-earth "Grandpa": a childlike, adult "innocence of becoming", a valiant naivety and a rebellious wisdom of the heart.

Or to put it another way: How could someone write with such empathy and inner authenticity if they had never experienced, suffered and experienced first-hand what they are writing about? For me, it's inconceivable. A book like this can only be written by someone who can empathise with these and similar worries and hardships; someone who had had their own experiences on this level and had learned from life.

And that's why, in the end, I left the whole Little Tree passage in our correspondence. Just with this important, long addition. I also put the word 'fictional' wherever I mentioned 'Indian'. Because, as I said, it is not an authentic Indian story, but a fictionalised Rousseauist story ...

---

6   Ibid.
7   See: Rutger Bregman: Humankind – a Hopeful History, London 2020

Rudolf Gaßenhuber   March 29, 2024

Dear Robert

Thank you for your meticulous examination of the Little Tree text with regard to racist slurs. There is nothing of the sort. It is hard to believe that Asa Carter, a widely known racist, wrote such a text. This total transformation does indeed look like a switch from Saul to Paul, like a conversion to the good. But I don't think that's the case here, we're not seeing a conversion, but an inner, partial change of sides, so to speak, a coming to light of hidden, even forbidden, probably also hated parts of oneself. Little Tree does not describe what it was like, but how many – and even some nasty racists – secretly wished it had been.

The US historian Dan T. Carter had been studying the phenomenon of Asa and Forrest Carter (1925-1979) for decades and finally published his book on the subject in 2023, "Unmasking the Klansman: The Double Life of Asa and Forrest Carter" (Athens 2023). On January 18, 2024, he gave a lecture on "The Double Life of Asa Carter"[8]. The lecture describes Asa Carter's life from World War II participant as a sailor at the age of 18 to the racist speechwriter for the politician George Wallace, the writer of the book "Gone to Texas" – which was made into a film as "The Outlaw Josey Wales" (1976), a revenge film with a peaceful ending, starring Clint Eastwood – and of the book "The Education of Little Tree" (1976). Dan T. Carter doesn't see a real transformation anywhere, but a racist throughout, who also said to have written Little Tree just for the money. At the end of the lecture, an audience member asks: "Was there a true cathartic moment for Asa Carter, did he really change, was there any change in sentiment?" Carter answers no, many would have wished it, but it wasn't like that and he reports that just a few days before his death he had racially abused a black couple in the worst possible way[9].

How can we understand this, how to deal with it? I would like to outline an answer that seems plausible to me. Surprisingly, an open-heartedness and a lively intuition, even a sense of heart, remained alive in Asa Carter. As Forrest Carter, he is consistently portrayed as friendly and likeable.

---

8   See https://www.youtube.com/watch?v=gf2CtILoewk
9   See https://www.youtube.com/watch?v=gf2CtILoewk from minute 50:40–52:40, accessed March 29, 2024

From this emotional source he was able to feel and write Little Tree. I suspect that here he was able to indulge in a warmth that he otherwise fought within himself, numbed it with alcohol, destroyed it with violence. Cursing, fighting and hurting somebody helps to numb one's own soft inside. Fully developed in the book Little Tree – and also to some extend in the ultimate willingness of the film character Josey Wales to make peace – the gentle found its expression, which the fictional character Forrest Carter could allow, but Asa Carter had to massively reject. Asa Forrest Carter unites in himself a deep divisiveness that also manifests itself in the USA until today as an imperial world ruler of war and secret admirer of Indian universal humanity, sovereignty and closeness to nature.

Asa Carter was a special person, one of those rare characters who could more or less unite the contradictions of his life, or rather the contradictions of USA, in a single person. He was both a peace-loving Indian friend and a hard-core racist. As Dan T. Carter supposes, one key to the emergence of his hardened, fearful, and violent racist side may lie in the severe humiliation he experienced at the age of 18. He, the brilliant student and graduate, failed the entrance exam for officer training in mathematics. It was just enough for a third-class seaman in the navy during the Second World War. Presumably, deeper wounds occurred much earlier in his Methodist home, but I know nothing about this. In general, one must assume that deep injuries to self-confidence and self-acceptance lead to an armor of fear and a readiness to use violence. Asa Carter, 1959 on AM Radio Broadcast: "Make No Mistake. The introduction of vast numbers of Mexicans and other colored people is a recipe for racial suicide. White Christian America will not survive such an onslaught ..."[10]. The fear of strangers, the fear of crime, of unrest, the loss of livelihood, the fear of losing one's own identity, such fears are tamed by a corset of violence and transformed into a feigned strength and apparent security.

As this story was penned by a real racist and xenophobe, so what do we think of Little Tree? I would say that an unlived life breaks through here, not liveable in his reality, only liveable in the self-invention of "Forrest Carter". Tender, childlike, unadulterated because not lived out feelings that have never grown a hard shell and can therefore express themselves all the more movingly and touchingly. Here speaks an innocent, unspoiled child, a sympathetic Forrest Carter, who must of course be immediately dragged

---

10   Ibid. at min. 29:00

back into the mud by Asa Carter, who would only have written it for money. In my opinion, the revelation of this split character makes the story of Little Tree all the more interesting, all the more genuine, all the more real. It is precisely through this refraction that the USA readership can get closer to emotions that are otherwise heavily laden with taboo and guilt. Normally such a text would be esoteric outsider literature. Only through the connection with its opposite does it become readable and sensitive for many.

The book Little Tree sold 200,000 copies between 1979 and 1989; and it was only when the New York Times published the exposé "Transformation of a Klansman" by Dan T. Carter in 1991 that the figures exploded to 800,000. People love scandals, but they also love the twilight, the unclear identities, the mix-ups, the play with roles and masks behind which, as in a good joke, something forbidden or hidden can be addressed or hinted at. Psychologically speaking, "Forrest Carter" is an ingenious trick to be allowed to live something as an invented role that an Asa Carter would have absolutely hated, where everything soft is despised as weak, unmanly and cowardly. Throughout his life, Asa Carter represents "segregation yesterday, segregation today, segregation always", as he put it in a famous speech for George Wallace. Forrest Carter, however, represents the USA's secret love and admiration for the peoples that they have successively destroyed in the long years of the Indian wars instead of integrating them and their wisdom into their lives.

Dear Robert, we have just spoken on the phone on March 31, 2024 and you mentioned that this violent inner conflict reminded you of Nietzsche, who even broke down and went insane because of it. He, the icy one, the master man, was flooded with compassion in Turin in 1889 at the sight of a horse being cruelly beaten by the coachman, and he embraced the horse in tears. For Nietzsche, his mental decline culminated in an eleven-year-long derangement. He did not speak another word after this event until his death. When his old friend Overbeck visited him soon afterwards to help him, Nietzsche recognized him, rushed towards him, burst into tears, only to sink back immediately onto the sofa in convulsions.

Can we compare the two events in the lives of Carter and Nietzsche, in both cases a cold, hard shell was broken – or was it shed like a snakeskin in the case of Asa Carter – and had another empathetic, compassionate side emerged? You know Nietzsche better than I do, I can only give you a working hypothesis of psychological connections. The two overall images have certain overlaps, a tender, wounded and unlived side is shielded by a hard shell of greatness and invulnerability. The nature of the breakthrough and also the extent of the friendliness that breaks through the shell are, of course, very different.

Nietzsche was certainly not a racist or anti-Semite, but he was definitely someone who was electrified and emotionally uplifted by the differences among people, between the lower and the higher. In his 1887 essay "On the Genealogy of Morality", he writes: "The pathos of nobility and distance, as I said, the permanent and dominant overall and basic feeling of a higher ruling species in relation to a lower species, to a 'below' – that is the origin of the opposition of 'good' and 'bad'."[11] This "pathos of distance", the intoxicating feeling of superiority, runs through his youth and his entire life, it makes the highly gifted person an eccentric – and it always lifts him up. His real life gives ample reason for this, it is marked by loneliness, lack of understanding, beatings from his father, unkindness, illness, early death of his father, lifelong dependence on his mother and scheming sister, a complete lack of fulfilling, even physical love, deep loneliness, betrayal, repeated bouts of headaches from a young age, consistent lack of success in his writings and repeated illness and loneliness. The discrepancy between the high and proud tone of his writings and his real, one might even say miserable, life is appalling and actually heartbreaking. What a tension! How much strength does it require, what a hard reversal is needed in order to pull oneself up again and again from the real malaise into "higher spheres". This is my trace, so to speak, massive inner conflicts that could have led to mental breakdown and could also have promoted a brain tumor.

How is this upswing even possible? I think that appropriate suffering and compassion for oneself and others is replaced here by the firm and often practiced belief in a fictitious triumph hoped for in the distant future. Nietzsche pulls himself out of the swamp, intoxicating himself with his own thoughts and words, just as his many readers did and do years later. A feeling of pride is immediately felt and supersedes compassion. For example, in 1885 he wrote to Heinrich Köselitz alias Peter Gast: "Noble is the doubt about the shareability of the heart; solitude not as chosen, but as given."[12]

---

11   Friedrich Nietzsche: On the Genealogy of Morality, First Essay: 'Good and Evil', 'Good and Bad', section 2, London 1897, translated by W. A. Hausemann, https://archive.org/details/GenealogyOfMorals

12   http://www.zeno.org/Philosophie/M/Nietzsche,+Friedrich/Briefe/1885/199.+An+Peter+Gast,+23.8.1885

The lack of empathic understanding, suffered deeply throughout his life, is seen almost as inevitable, then exaggerated as distanced nobility. The real pain is numbed by an intoxication of fictitious heights. Why Nietzsche takes this path, why secure attachment, freedom from shame and loneliness were hardly attainable for him from childhood onwards, until finally only the path of compensation seems feasible to him, would be a worthwhile investigation in its own right. Since the book "Thus Spoke Zarathustra" from 1883–1885, Nietzsche has, in my opinion, moved completely into this fictional, heroic sphere; it is his self-apotheosis after the life crisis surrounding Lou Salomé, Paul Rée and his own family. Zarathustra speaks: "Of what account is my happiness!" answered he, "I have long ceased to strive any more for happiness, I strive for my work."[13] Later he described himself in a letter as a philosopher "who had no present and didn't actually want one."[14]

A "pathos of distance" is a stark contrast to empathic participation. In reality, however, empathic participation would often be what is appropriate, what appeals to us. If what is appealing is notoriously ignored and replaced by something else, like distance and self-aggrandizement, we live a false self. In Nietzsche's case, it is specifically the needy parts of himself in the desire for empathy and unconditional acceptance that could not be lived, were devalued and dismissed in himself and others. The horse scene strikes his life like a flash of compassion, and suddenly he presumably recognized himself in this carriage horse: lonely, always struggling and yet beaten. Pity for the horse and himself breaks out. With the increasing disintegration of his personality, the unlived life can no longer be ignored and transformed into something hard and proud. If this was the case, then, tragically, it was only at the moment of mental death that real life somehow manifested itself.

In this scene, Nietzsche can also be seen as a representative of modern man, who not only presumes to be the master of himself, but also the master of nature. From this view compassion for the beaten horse causes a rift in the distance to the maltreated creature, a deviation from the modern path of untouchability. Milan Kundera saw it this way and I would like to quote the passage to you in context:

13　Friedrich Nietzsche: Thus Spoke Zarathustra, LXI. The Honey Sacrifice, https://www.gutenberg.org/files/1998/1998-h/1998-h.htm

14　Venice, October 22, 1887: Letter to Hans von Bülow. http://www.thenietzschechannel.com/correspondence/eng/nlett-1887.htm

"Tereza keeps appearing before my eyes. I see her sitting on the stump petting Karenin's head [a dog, R.G.] and ruminating on mankind's débâcles. Another image also comes to mind: Nietzsche leaving his hotel in Turin. Seeing a horse and a coachman beating it with a whip, Nietzsche went up to the horse and, before the coachman's very eyes, put his arms around the horse's neck and burst into tears.

That took place in 1889, when Nietzsche, too, had removed himself from the world of people. In other words, it was at the time when his mental illness had just erupted. But for that very reason I feel his gesture has broad implications: Nietzsche was trying to apologize to the horse for Descartes. His lunacy (that is, his final break with mankind) began at the very moment he burst into tears over the horse.

And that is the Nietzsche I love, just as I love Tereza with the mortally ill dog resting his head in her lap. I see them one next to the other: both stepping down from the road along which mankind, 'the master and proprietor of nature', marches onward."[15]

The fact that Kundera "loves" Nietzsche may sound strange here; here a person goes mad and is taken away from others. He is almost completely dehumanised. Well, at the same time he regains some of his vitality, but also in a terrible form, in an isolated outburst. Stepping down from the "road of the master and proprietor of nature" as such cannot be the solution, that is not enough. The empathic, new, non-detached life would also have to find a new human form.

Forrest Carter was granted the privilege of taking a comparatively large step forward here. In the story of Little Tree, he described the seed, an even childlike beginning of a good, different life that may have a presence throughout all adversity.

Warm regards

Rudolf

[End of Interim remarks. Addendum from the years 2023–2024]

---

15   Milan Kundera: The Unbearable Lightness of Being, London & Boston 2000, p. 282

7.

Rudolf Gaßenhuber March 12, 2017

Dear Mr. Kozljanič

you express exactly what I feel. I can nothing else but agree, the "forces leading to sources of life are called for, scoops from the wells of child memories and a skilful and patient cultivation of the sense of heart." What you describe with a lot of sentiment and appropriate pathos, that's it, this constitutes the friendship with nature and exactly characterizes the sense of heart, which means that "the world ... responded to me as well." When we address things, they lose their status of objects and become "beings" – in a way or another, but in any case something that is not dead, not only matter, and they emanate something that can appeal to me. – The sense of heart can be evolved like the musical ear or the sense of touch. Or as Little Tree so nicely told: "Granma said that the spirit mind was like any other muscle. If you used it it got bigger and stronger. She said the only way it could get that way was using it to understand, but you couldn't open the door to it until you quit being greedy and such with your body mind. The understanding commenced to take up, and the more you tried to understand, the bigger it got. Natural, she said, understanding and love was the same thing"[1]. – With this writing and Little Tree you have summarized and rounded last year's key feeling.

The other way round it can be said that without this muscle, without the willingness to empathy and love there is no genuine contact with the world. In your words we can say that "friendship with nature without an open or reopened access to crucial life sources is not possible." Yes, without resonance and love there is no real contact, everything remains more or less strange, as if being behind a glass pane. We can see through it, but

---

[1] Forrest Carter: The Education of Little Tree, Albuquerque 1986, p. 60

we cannot feel it. The glass breaks when the sense of heart opens. Glass is cold, hard and brittle – quite similar to the space of perception of estranged life. In Grimm's fairy tale 'The Seven Ravens' the brothers are cursed, transformed into ravens henceforth living in a Glass Mountain. But only through their sister's love and a connecting ring, they are liberated. They succeed to live up to the bygone, inner wealth of life. The wealth of human life consists in being appealed – something appeals to me or responds to me. However, these words are deceitful. I wanted to write "things mean something to me", but this sounds like an intellectual association. When being appealed I do not mean the intellectual associations I have (they are part of it), but being touched and somehow deeply moved. The emotions do not have to be very strong. The crucial point is the connection between me and the other one. How can I tell the difference between (intellectual, aesthetic) associations and real resonance? Martin Buber coined this strong phrase: "All actual life is encounter." What is encounter? It is an unreserved admittance and mutual responsiveness, in other words: encounter is the opposite of loneliness. We can stay lonely in our associations but not in the lived sense of heart. Nature receives him and speaks to him as it is told in your beautiful Indian story: "The pines whispered and the wind picked up, and they commenced to sing, 'Little Tree is home … Little Tree is home!" (p. 203). The loneliness and the pain have been overcome – like at the beginning of the story: The five-year-old lost his mother and misses her, he feels so lonely. His grandmother sings a welcome song, the woods and the wind, the creek and the deer, the quail-hen and the crow welcome him. And his ties are restored. "They now have sensed him coming / […] / 'Brave is the heart of Little Tree / And kindness is his strength' […]". "Granma sang and rocked slowly back and forth. And I could hear the wind talking and Lay-nah, the spring branch, singing about me and telling all my brothers." (p. 5) And there must be witnesses of rebirth, of course, others, those who share and experience it in a similar way, yes, it is important: "The hounds knew and come closer around me and laid down, content with the feeling" (p. 203) – Beautiful.

Signs and superstition

Witnesses, symbols, reassurances … are a big topic of religious practice, a big topic of abuse (of power) that we have touched on already. Who needs the symbol, who is connected, who does it read? What is first the connection or the symbol? "Wind tore down a light pole and the orphanage was dark. I knew they had heard" (p. 193). He was well again, he was fine, and then he saw the "symbol" and took the event for a symbol. Now he knows it; it was a secret before and completely uncertain, when, how and if a symbol at all could show up, because first there is the connection and then the symbol appears. Little Tree does not know whether a symbol will show up, and he does not know what it will be like. He is unsure what to pay attention to. He watches out for the dog star (Sirius), his oak tree, for everything. Later religious practice by contrast adheres to the "symbols" and not to the connections. Religious practice believes to know the symbols beforehand, it reads the liver or throws bones, it reads in a book where the symbols and words are fixed forever. But for Little Tree a unique, irrevocable sign appears in the very moment of connection. I consider it to be very important; a unique "symbol" is an event in a given situation, always new, similar to encounter, and yet recognizable and comprehensible. Philosophers have established that "Individuum est ineffabile", the individual is beyond conception (ineffable), but neither for Little Tree nor for the sense of heart, which turns towards the individual as such. Getting in touch with the actual reality below the cult, below different notions, below scientific laws. – And there are recurrent symbols, inherent everyday phenomena, which are experienced as symbols in the moment of reconnection. If the connection re-establishes, the whole world can speak again. God, for instance, speaks to Job out of the thunderstorm and the harmonious and grand beauty of nature.

Brothers and patriarchs

Job's God, however, is an almighty Creator God who demands submission; Job's reconnection after his despair is subordination to the omnipotence of God and it corresponds to the understanding in his own tininess (Book of Job, chapter 38). Little Tree, however, connects himself at eye level and in amity with his brothers. This is what I want to express by contrasting a religion of awe and a religion of joy. Admittedly both establish a connection, but Little Tree's religion ignores the "seriousness of religious authority" in a patriarchal sense. It is not a religion of fear and obedience. His brotherhood with animals and nature is not without seriousness but entirely without disparagement and humiliation. Christianity as seen by Rudolf Otto and others is a version of a patriarchal religion based on enfeeblement and subordination. –

In my last letter I meant to say: In the vision quests you quoted, thank God (!), there is not a mix of shiver and fascination; these vision quests are examples of religious experience showing that the authoritarian notion of religion is but a specific form of religion. A 're-ligion', a re-connection via joy and brotherhood, is a 're-ligion' in its deepest sense, even if – or because – it does not work with fear, awe and the subordination to an omnipotent power. – As far as connection and subordination are concerned you will find more below.

Religion

Well, here is a necessary remark to the topic of "religion". Re-connection as the meaning of "religion" is not the origin of the word but a postulation. According to Cicero (106-43 B.C.) religion goes back to "relegere" which literally means "to read again, to pick up again, to put together again", figuratively "to consider, to pay attention to". Cicero was thinking of the temple cult, which had to be carefully observed. This religion (as conscientious adherence to rules handed down) of the cult of that time stood for him in contrast to the superstition of those days. One could say that here a cult and handling with symbols is contrasted against another handling with symbols. The Early Christian Doctor of the Church Lactantius (250–320 A.D.) tried the famous derivation from Latin "relegare" (instead of "relegere"), in his case to the Christian God. Etymologically a wrong track, but for religious people it would be just too nice if religion had this leap of meaning concerning connection. People love returning home, personal ties, the end of night and loneliness. But the question is where do we return home to, what are our ties, are they with a Creator God behind everything or rather with a world that can be experienced including all other creatures? That is not all. In a mystical experience there is the lived knowledge of oneness with the universe. Therefore one can say that there are two true religions, religions I can accept: Little Tree's brotherhood with nature and its creatures and a fusion with the universe. Both religions would be connections and encounters with every living thing and the living thing in general. For we may hope that we all are connatural in our intrinsicality with the universe "closely related" as you put it. – However, what became reality in the history of human life was the religion in Cicero's version of the term "relegere", the exact observance of cultic rules. This abandonment of experiencing and the orientation towards the fearful observance of actions unfortunately characterizes humans in general sometimes more, sometimes less and not just monotheists. Thus we have to admit that mankind in its religiosity has hardly got beyond the stage of superstition.

The drawback

Little Tree – a touching and an infinitely sad story. It is sad not because all those he loves die, but because also the world has long been dying from where this life originated. You wrote: "They lived alone in the mountains of Tennessee, hundreds of kilometres in the East away from the new homeland of the displaced Cherokee Indians. In any case, the old tribal union was more or less destroyed. Almost nothing was left from the old life." The former Indian life did not exist any longer, after Wounded Knee there were no free tribes ... Or Willow John: "Granpa said that long ago, Willow John had gone to the Nations. He had walked the mountains, and would not ride a car or train. He was gone three years and came back; but he would not talk of it. He would only say there was no Nation." (p. 147).

Go-khla-yeh called Geronimo
with bow and arrow,
1829–1909, chief warrior
of the Apache until 1886,
photograph of 1909

Why does Willow John have these dead eyes? Why Geronimo? Here we meet the back of the human race: Fury, hate, war and destruction. Since de Narváez (1528) and de Soto (1540) American Indians have been robbed, pillaged, proselytized, infected with diseases and enslaved by Europeans. Souls, gold and slaves once was the motto of Cortés, Pizarro, de Soto and many others, a fanatical, fundamentalist and later a social Darwinist legitimised raid. Columbus already promised his queen as much gold and slaves as she liked. In Peru Spanish conquistadors robbed and pillaged with utmost unscrupulous methods. In the three centuries that followed 300t of gold and 25,000t of silver, for example, were shipped to Spain ... a long trace of destruction and pillage through an entire continent.

Enlightenment

Historically Rousseau was a very significant impulse, of course. It was a first step towards a more appreciative access to foreign cultures. Being full of prejudice himself and everything but an ethnologist, he was nevertheless the first one not to look for the beginnings of humans in myths and the Bible, but in the history of mankind as a hunter and gatherer! This was literally a true sensation, a perception, an emergence from a prison of ideas and a first although timid attempt of contacting reality and its history. In this respect Rousseau's significance can be hardly overestimated. It was a beginning at the end of which the "others" were not merely perceived as slaves, servants, barbarians and Goths, red and yellow devils, but simply as our relatives. So Claude Lévi-Strauss could tell about Rousseau: "He is the father of us all."[2] And justly so, for without Rousseau's view indigenous peoples and human historicality would not have got into the focus of interest. But nonetheless we have to free ourselves from Rousseau for three reasons:

A) The image of savages he depicts is a complete distortion and depreciation of highly cultivated peoples and communities. So he writes about the savage: "His desires do not reach beyond his physical needs." "His soul cannot be touched by anything and just leaves itself to the mere feeling of present existence ..." – an animal-like, vague, identitarian condition. Rousseau remains the philosopher of the Enlightenment, i.e., he is deeply convinced of the superiority of his culture and era.

B) This disparaging image of the savage did not simply become effective but was distorted into an Rousseauistic ideal. The slogan "Back to Nature" (this slogan was attributed to Rousseau, but is not found in his

---

2   See also my co-authored chapter:
     https://de.wikipedia.org/wiki/Naturvolk#Begriffsgeschichte

works) became a dream place for all unfulfilled ideas of cultural criticism: relationship with nature, naturalness, sexuality, freedom from domination, community spirit, peace, silence ... depreciation as well as idealization, both are avoidances. In this sense Rousseau resp. the subsequently idealising and Rousseauistic view on indigenous peoples practised later distorts the view on true indigenous peoples.

Indigenous peoples on the other hand certainly are exemplary in many respects, but not in all. This is what I meant when saying we have "to free ourselves from Rousseau and take a closer look."

C) Besides the raging ignorance even among educated people is a mystery to me. When Rousseau wrote his essay about inequality in 1755, detailed travel reports from the New World, for instance by Cabeza de Vaca and Bartolomé de las Casas, had been accessible for 200 years in Europe, also quite popular and printed in many editions as part of the "Leyende negra" – the anti-Spanish propaganda. De Vaca, for example, describes in his "Shipwrecks" eight year long wanderings, from Florida to the Pacific Ocean to Mexico in 1528. He got in touch with dozens of Indian tribes and tried to make his living as a merchant and healer. He was a Catholic and not an ethnologist, but he still delivers a more realistic image of these peoples than the arrogant brainchilds of many an enlightener. Bluntly said, with all due respect for universal philanthropy, it still was all about the own enhancement and the triumph of the own group in Europe. In the US Capitol Dome Rotunda in Washington hangs a great painting about Hernando de Soto, a robber baron and looter by trade, all the way through Florida, North Carolina right up to the Mississippi – in the tale of American history, however, his expedition is viewed as the beginning of a great triumph over the indigenous peoples[3].

Back to the sense of heart I

How can we accomplish this returning back? The force of Little Tree's heart is astounding. He overcomes loneliness (p. 5, 203) and later on a hard darkening after harsh mistreatment. He was traumatized and cut off: "I would not see the pictures they sent" (p. 193). And yet he can deal with

---

3   See also the article I mainly authored and notably the last chapter concerning the historic importance of the battle: https://de.wikipedia.org/wiki/Schlacht_von_ Mauvilla, also as Addendum at the end of this letter.

all that with the help of his grandparents, the help of his old oak tree, and others. – How can we generally succeed? We have already talked a lot about the biographic and psychological opening of the heart and the world, little about the social and cultural side. You mentioned the "cultivation of just wrath" and about "the preferably realistic belief in humanity", about "even under these circumstances", about "nonetheless" and about "ethical tolerance". There is a lot of contradiction, a struggle, a desire, and a cherished 'however' that wants to stay open and permeable after all. Well I think, the same happens to all those who still bear a burning flame inside. Hard but gentle, ready to fight and yet affectionate, realistic and yet positive. – Two years ago I wrote a longer essay on this subject, enclosed as a PDF file[4]. It is quite a dense text, it takes the reader to the dark human abysses of recent history and invites the reader to mentally go along. The equation of comprehension and love reaches its limits. The text means very much to me. To me it was a liberation from the mildew, in the sense of leading a life according to the principles of Adorno, which had laid itself on the soul of many people of the present generation. So this text still appeals to me. The Hitler passages about violence and obedience are dark, for sure, but in a way the text manages to reach an exit at least to the verge of the Hades. This is why I would like to send it to you. Your passage in the letter "cultivation of love and also cultivation of just wrath" directly inspired me. Yes, the sense of heart is not everything, it is just a part at best, often withered, numb that sort of thing. And on the other hand it has not been placed into a cordial world either. You are characterizing the atmosphere around Helene Stöcker with these words: almost "in despair about her ideals and deeply depressed, she wrote after the outbreak of World War I in 1914: 'If we could not hope that human love and goodness become reality some time, then we don't want to live such a life. This is the meaning of life, at least for me'." – How can we live and lead a decent life, when facing a total war, hatred and destruction?

Back to the sense of heart II

In the announcement of her book in 1924, Helene Stöcker suggests an answer to the horror: "It finally aims – and perhaps above all – at bridging the chasms between humans based on the tragic recognition of

---

4   Published in book form: Rudolf Gaßenhuber: Herzsinn und Weltangst,
    Philosophisch-psychologische Essays, München 2018

the 'irresponsibility of man for his being and his existence' to reach that ethical tolerance; it wants to achieve that supreme form of justice towards human imperfection which means 'love with one's eyes open'!" In your own words you add with the goal: "The attempt requiring patience, trust, and a spirit of conciliation despite the irresponsibility and shortcomings of humans and to help – together with them! – shape a more human future". – These are difficult topics that can probably be represented in a different way after 1945. In my book "Herzsinn und Weltangst" mentioned above, I partly chose to go a different way. I will gladly discuss it with you. Please, allow me to present a third approach. In a film worth seeing on Martin Buber[5] Buber presents himself as a "man of hope" relentless in his endeavour of understanding and conciliation. But why didn't he deal with the "other psychology" as they say in the film – that of the roots of revengefulness and thirst for glory? Were people then simply relieved that it was over, and were they no longer ready for it? Buber's attitude results in a lack of knowledge: "I always ask myself wherefrom? Then I conceive the idea ... of a certain historic crisis of the German people that I barely comprehend." We can ask ourselves, why could the master of dialogism not grasp the opposite of dialogue better? – Thus three positions that can be perhaps marked in this way: My approach to a problem: revulsion plus fading out plus sense of heart; Helene Stöcker: Wrath plus love with seeing eyes plus hope; Martin Buber: Understandably exhausted pushing aside of inhuman aspects plus hope.

Sources or compromises

Your demand to see nature as the future really surprised me. When thinking about nature as the history of nature and man, it appears to me in a wide arc as a finite history. With its advanced civilizations and an expanding communization mankind has broken up the cycle of life and bent it up to a line of growth. Like a slant saw slightly held downwards, it runs upwards over many teeth of new progress but altogether points into the opposite direction. Earlier generations of humans lived in the eternal cycles of nature and were part of them, but such a form of existence is no longer attainable for us. Indians "were" the buffaloes, they "were" the forests – we the modern ones, however, stand for efficiency and control, a

---

5   „Martin Buber, Religionsphilosoph und Humanist" documentary France 2015, arte, http://programm.ard.de/?sendung=2872418727217065

state and taxes. The cultural layer becomes excessively dominant, nature becomes the leftover, the remaining other thing, a place of longing, the lost paradise. Lately the Garden of Eden is readily located as a historical event in the Mesopotamian area, referred to as a society of hunters and gatherers. I do think, these were paradises, the happy lasting periods of hundreds of thousands of years of this life form. – But the heart of these children still lives within us: "But above all when the throb was warm, loving, enthusiastic, passionate and longing. For in these moments we were very close to our innermost, most individual and creative centre; a creative centre that is closely related to the creative centre of the world." That is a very beautiful, deep and comforting idea. I also hope that we may think this way that creation means love and humans, for instance, are conceived out of love, and that this parental love is the basis of each life. With this in mind, we can and have to speak about the sources of life, of course. In your own words: "These sources are free and complimentary and are like gushing springs: They constantly throw themselves away on you." Yes, the archetype of it is the sun and its undoubted life-giving generosity. In spiritual experiencing it is the self-giving, pure love, "human love and goodness ... the meaning of life" (Stöcker). It is joy, richness of life, and integrity – and by no means a compromise.

In this spirit I wish you a fresh and sunny springtime and will be glad to hear from you again.

Warm regards

R. G.

Addendum

Here you will find the text of the article in case the Wikipedia site – with all its images and cross-references – is not accessible: https://de.wikipedia.org/wiki/Schlacht_von_Mauvilla

Historical importance of the Mauvilla battle

Provided the figures given by the Spanish are correct the Mauvilla battle of 1540 with more than two thousand deaths probably was the biggest battle that has ever been fought on North-American ground up to that time. It marks the gory conquest of North America's Southeast, which found its end with the Jamestown massacre of 1662 and the Powhatan wars in 1664. As a result the Powhatan tribe was destroyed, the Southeast Indians became widely wiped out by wars and pestilence.

In terms of North America the battle marks the beginning of a long series of battles until the massacre at Wounded Knee in 1890 – thus the beginning of Indian wars in North America.

The European assessment of these events has been fluctuating ever since between the far apart poles of "ruthless crime and genocide" and "the beginning of a glorious discovery and successful opening of the American continent". In the 16th century already we can find detailed and passionate accusations of the injustices and cruelties made by eyewitnesses of the conquests and the first historians of the New World: Las Casas, Cabeza de Vaca, Girolami Benzoni, Theodor de Bry and others. The following special criticism concerning the allegedly particularly cruel and bloodthirsty Spanish-Catholic conquests, the notion of 'Leyenda negra' (Black Legend), became a propaganda tool in the conflict against the Spanish dominance in the centuries to follow. Today Howard Zinn, Tsvetan Todorov and many others hold a similarly critical and condemning view on the destructive wars against Indian peoples. – At the summit of glorious conquests and triumphant victories 16th century Francisco López de Gómara and 18th century Adam Smith can be named as representative for many. In his book "The Wealth of Nations" the latter wrote: "The discovery of America and that of a passage to the East Indies by the Cape of Good Hope are the two greatest events registered by the history of humanity." Both contrary assessments can be illustrated such as: On top a wall painting in the Palacio Nacional (Mexico) by Diego Rivera: "The Arrival of Hernan Cortez in Veracruz" with its topic of cruel oppression by the Spaniards and below the monumental painting in the U.S. Capitol Rotunda by William Henry Powell "The Discovery of the Mississippi" with its topic of the triumphant arrival of Hernando de Soto emphasized by submissively receiving Indians.

An originally Indian view of the events is partly opposite to these two assessments. In both assessments Europeans are placed on top of the social hierarchy, Indians are placed below, once as the oppressed and once as the admirers of the white man. In the Indian reality, however, the attitude changes with the experience. Hence the white man is admired at the beginning and sometimes even considered immortal like God. In the further course events disillusionment sets in. The Spaniards are experienced as barbarians who destroy their sacred sites, they behave as liars and cheats. The Inca king

Manco Inca accuses the Spaniards: They have "done bad things to us by taking away our possessions, our women, our sons, our daughters, our fields, our food, and many other things we had in our lands in a violent and fraudulent way against our will." With Georg Christoph Lichtenberg's ironic expression we can therefore rightly say: "The American who first discovered Columbus made an evil discovery." In a picture this Indian perception of the hateful white man can be illustrated, for instance, with the triumph against general Custer. Custer lies dead on the ground as a red figure, an Indian victory of defining importance.

The three pictures are next to the Wikipedia article with the following captions:

The wall painting by Diego Rivera in the National palace in Mexico City illustrates the oppression by the Spaniards after the arrival of Hernan Cortez in Veracruz.

One of the eight large format historical paintings inside the Capitol Rotunda in Washington, an idealizing illustration of the superb arrival of Spaniards at the Mississippi after the Mauvilla battle.

Battle at Little Bighorn in 1876 painted by Indian chief and battle participant Kicking Bear in 1898, one of the few victories of Indians over the white man.

Rudolf Gaßenhuber   June 1, 2017

Dear Mr. Kozljanič

with some resonance and a certain distance I would like to return to the beginning of our exchange of ideas and to your book "Friendship with Nature". I want to make a summary, what have I learnt, what do I see more clearly after this year? Your book ends with these thoughts: "Our Western history of mind starts with the point that the 'mythical spirit' of our ancestors, who once were indigenous peoples themselves, has been 'overcome' and replaced by what we call 'Geist' (spirit) namely lógos, nous. And it is exactly this history of mind, our history of world conquest by lógos, which poses in its wake massive problems today."[1] I think, it is the fragile difference between life and thinking, nature and spirit, the eternal task of modern self-reflection, which became clearer to me through your book and our letters.

One could object now, is it really the spirit that causes problems, is the spirit not rather a means of dominating nature and technology a great promoter of human life, and is an inquiring mind not a benefactor of knowledge and deep joy in the world? So is it not the spirit we put too much into the focus as the disparaging force of life within nature, but our striving for power and the dominance over nature? The spirit, isn't it just a tool that becomes a problem due to its application? We have to ask more exactly what happens if the spirit is put into the focus before science, technology, control prevail and are also violently applied?

---

1   Robert Josef Kozljanič: Freundschaft mit der Natur – Naturphilosophische Praxis und Tiefenökologie, Klein Jasedow 2008, p. 137

I want to verify the question with Martin Buber as a witness beyond suspicion of a monotheistic religion and admirer of the spiritual. Why above suspicion, because as a philosopher of genuine encounter and common humanity, he does not underlie the suspicion but enjoys a reputation of a philosopher of consistent *joie de vivre*. Is it possible to exemplify our distance towards nature and our remoteness from real life, which has almost completely slid into self-evidence, by reference to Martin Buber?

For Buber the world is bipartite into an It-World of things, objects and use and into a Thou-World of meeting, interpersonal relations and spirit. The distinction resembles the comparison between nature and spirit, albeit Buber's It-World is not nature in the proper sense of the word but a reified nature as an object of grasping, science, and technology. He disparages primordial nature and enhances the spirit, as we can see here – but one by one.

Under the term of nature I rather understand the manifold, entire present beyond cities and civilization, for instance in the following experience I had. Lately I was at the seaside and briefly wrote the following down:

Was just at the beach in the morning. Mild sun, quiet water and an endless variety of light waves, water waves, sand waves scurrying, waving, and lasting. I splash through the water, a crab attacks me, wants to expel me from its territory, I hold out my hand to him, he "pokes" me. It ripples, splashes and waves, sand and seashells everywhere. What more could one want? What spirit, conversation, knowledge or a Thou are good for? Of course, the crab was a small opponent, a little fighter and player. But the whole thing is not a Thou. It is simply lovely. The wonderful world as it is for us, and which we fit into so well, not only aesthetically yet in a comprehensive way right up to the carefree, related, united, attentive almost thoughtless presence. It is so lovely here.

Is this somehow a lesser "It-World", a world that would not be so rich like a genuine conversation, like the spirit? Meeting a Thou may happen later and be fulfilling. But no doubt there are diverse atmospheres, and in my opinion it would be a bad sacrilege to arrange them according to "perfection" and "nearness to God". The evil of such claim of truth religions not only lies in the disparagement, exclusion and persecution of heretics or dissenters, but in the same thirst for hierarchy, and not seldom the servile order becomes apparent concerning feelings and human abilities: Some are depreciated others are favoured.

From nature to the object

Thus Buber's world, for instance, is based from the beginning on an external, quasi contemporary-experimental notion of experience. The experienced human confronts the world, he is not part of it and could then say: "It is lovely here". Buber's experienced human looks at the world like a scientist. Buber writes: "It is said that man experiences his world. What does that mean? Man travels the surface of the things and experiences them. He gets from them a knowledge of their nature, an experience. ... The experiencer has no share in the world."[2] Hereby everything has been actually said and decided. "Experience" is reduced to the examination of things. Experience does not encompass being in a certain situation, neither joy about things, the discovery, the astonishment, the rapt running about of children who find this and that, play at it, examine, move on. ... Buber starts from a distanced, separated face-to-face situation, from a scientist alienated from actual reality, whose sensorium is reduced to knowledge and research. So little wonder that this poor It-World must be urgently compensated as extensively as possible by a Thou-World, which partly attenuates the divide. For Buber the present, the fulfilled and real present only exists within the encounter and relation. He writes: "The present ... only exists in so far as actual presentness, encounter, and relation exist. The present arises only in virtue of the fact that the Thou becomes present." (p. 16)

Well is there no sea, no soil, no sky, no sun, no walking, standing, sitting on the ground, no existence in a given situation – the waves ripple or roar, the wind plays or gushes – does this not mean to be the present? Buber's famous formula: "All actual life is encounter" has to be extended on both sides. First, life is not a fleeting encounter, but also lasting sympathy, as well as the cosmos and the great order of nature. And second, real life is also any experience of real existence in the world like this formula: "Any real life lives in the entire present". The present I mean comprises everything that exists: earth, water, sky, sun, the crab and the Thou. Only with that the balance is preserved again, the human spirit, and the Thou, lógos and word would be a force field among others. The spirit would have abandoned his central position and regained its place within the diversity of living things.

---

2   Martin Buber: Ich und Du, Leipzig 1923, p. 9

From the sun to heaven's light

One can put it even more clearly: In the cosmologies of early empires the sun gradually disappears as an autonomous and world-shaping element, either it is controlled by human-like deities, created by a creator deity or simply left out! From now on four elements shape the world: water, fire, air and earth, the sun is no longer mentioned. In all monotheistic religions the sun is eventually faded out and replaced or covered by other things.

Typically so in Gnostic, Kabbalistic, and Hasidic religious movements, where the spirit is contrasted with nature. The antagonists are the spiritual and telluric forces, heaven's light, and earth fire, spirit and nature. Where the sun was, there is light, spirit, and reason. Where life force was, there is cognitive power. Where the sun was, heaven's light is shining now. Why does heaven's light better fit than the sun into this world increasingly dominated by humans? What is suddenly wrong with the sun? One can easily see it, light goes better with spirit, personal existence, perception, knowledge, understanding, and dominance. Light has a memorable equivalent in the awakening awareness and self-awareness of humans. All the way to the Enlightenment and the light of reason, it stands for clarity, the day, and human self-awareness and self-confidence. – The sun, however, transcends the space of perception. It gives us all the light that enables eyesight, but we cannot quietly observe it with the naked eye. Those who look into the sun, lower their glance, those who do it far too long risk to go blind. And yet the sun is rather a small thing in the world with its flat surface of the earth and the firmament we experience in comparison with the tremendous amount of earth, water and wind. It is tiny, not bigger than the moon in the sky and yet it shines on everything on earth. The sun determines whether it is day or night, summer or winter, whether everything thrives, freezes or withers. And it is the only thing that cannot be calmly looked at, except for quite terrible or embarrassing events when we turn away by instinct. The central life-giving entity eludes our eyes at the same time. For humans its realm in the sky is quasi taboo, they cannot take a sharp eye at it. The blue sky and the light in general is a completely different story. Well-dosed it is pleasant and opens the whole world. Anything that is well lit can be embraced, grasped, identified; here the overview, clarity, and control prevail. No doubt light corresponds much better to a programme of a comprehensive reason than a sun, which makes the absolute weakness and dependence of humans visible.

Where the sun existed before, there is the personal spirit in Judaism and Christianity, where life earlier emerged, arise spiritual enthusiasm and 'spiritus' now. The character of God shifts from a giver of life to an exciter of spiritual enthusiasm and joy. The witness of truth is now carried out through profound human capability. Divinity culminates in humans, it does not manifest itself any more equally in the life of all creatures, but especially in a concentrated form in the unification of spirit and nature in humans. God mutates from a God of life to a God of spirit, of reason (lógos), of word. God shrinks from a giver of life for all creatures to an authority for the unification of spirit and nature, which particularly manifests in humans. Now we say: Also our awareness wakes up every morning and enables perception, wakefulness and new unification of spirit and nature; in any form of insight and knowledge and successful solution, the happiness of unity of spirit and world is repeated.

Yet there is more to life, there is not Heaven's light only but also its cause. And the cause of Heaven's light shines for all creatures in their way, and makes them live on their own terms, in their own sense. Human spirit is a small and sometimes inspiring addition, but it is not life. – Hence this nice parallel: Spirit and life act like Heaven's light and sun. Heaven's light is clear and wide, consistent and mild, the sun, however, is super-bright and spotty, concentrated and burning. Therefore, as Heaven's light is a rather pale and soothing impact of the sun, the spirit is a clear, far sighted and pale progeny of life.

The sun is breaking through the fog

The trick of monotheism

The mythological detachment of the sun through the sky – together with the rise of cities and realms – is paralleled with a gradual shifting of the centre of nature's life towards a human-spiritual one. The change takes place over many transitions and intermediate forms and finally leads to a more striking difference: Previously the human being was a creature like all others and by no means something outstanding, on the contrary, animals were admired and adored. Now humans are in real terms and conceptually separated from animals and rated higher; the term "anthropocentrism" only mentions the central position, the revaluation is missing. A more explicit term would be "anthroparchy", the reign of humans in terms of his singularity, his cognitive capabilities, the reign of his human-spiritual force. One could say that it was a clever trick that monotheism tried to plant the human spirit on the world as a divine lógos. The word was said to be at the beginning, so God would have similarly reigned as he does with humans now, and in his comprehending spirit not only shows a unification with the world, but closeness with God. A similar lógos reigns everywhere, in God, in the world, and in humans. The "divine unity of spirit and nature"[3] appears among particularly called teachers and prophets in particular pureness, but every single individual is called to live this unity. This is the key of this new divinization: a current particularly human ability, the creative and meeting spirit is simultaneously viewed as the central quality of God. The new Spiritual God becomes a builder, potter, and eternal, personal counterpart. – Old nature religions conceived, imitated and were inspired by natural phenomena and animals. The new human distanced from nature is inspired by himself and by the world he created. He creates a new God who corresponds to his own capabilities and makes him godlike. The new God does not manifest himself in nature but prominently in holy texts. The script becomes the force field of the priestly word, where it can happen that the disciples "unite to a enthusiastic unity ... which indicates the divine centre of all being." (ibid. p. 27) Here we can see the new human world: In the centre of existence shall be enthusiasm, spirit, something that humans can also experience inside as the centre.

---

3   Martin Buber: Die Erzählungen der Chassidim, Zürich 1949, p. 33

Let's build ourselves a monotheism

So this is how it works, we pick some ability, some touching feeling and place it in the central position of everything. Instead of enthusiasm we could also support a quiet, dragging feeling of happiness and place it in the centre of the world and humans:

- God then manifests himself in the dawning of the morning, in the quiet sea after the night, in the beginning of the day, when the sun slowly emerges (in ancient Egypt Chepre the shining and shimmering scarab beetle that arises out of itself in the sands of the river Nile), in this warm, body close feeling that feels mild and quiet, just as the world shows itself. Here we are so very close to God, here God is in us.

- Or how about a God of love? Are we not connected with all ancestors and a life-family with all animals, connected with a cordial band and the sense of heart? The great chain of relationship reaches up to us and holds me as an element I bear inside. In the love of genders the entity of life manifests itself, the entire chain of life lives through love and stays alive. It is infatuation and love making new life coming into existence and passes life on. Life is love.

- Or how about the black jaguar whose power and suppleness we admire and whose deadly force makes us shiver; with the sun of the night, with passion and willingness to sacrifice; is it not blood and sacrifice which make life worth living and go along with a strong feeling of being alive?

- Or with a God of fear? Does our connectedness with the world as a whole not manifest at the strongest in our fear? When the weather god rumbles and strikes lightnings, when the god of war sets forth or the plague destroys life, when diseases make us understand what is important in life.

Many are the gods. All of them were already worshipped. Many things move us and can mean deep connectedness. But one thing is certain: In a poly-emotional world of various moods and atmospheres life is better and more genuine. Presently and diversely the new and the old is shown again and again through the opening of the heart towards us and towards the world. Monotheism and the supremacy of the spirit mean a depletion and extreme narrowing of living things, which close themselves to the present. This closeness and caginess means non-perception and exclusion. To a great extent the present is not experienced, connections are cut or ignored, life is not lived. Even any permanent exclusion becomes an adversary of the entire life. – There is at least hope for the opposite, we live for the entire present.

Friendship with nature

The focus on spirit and on the individual condensed in the Jewish-Greek-Christian cultural area has ultimately spread over the whole world. Even if there is no personal God for many of us, the image of the world and self-perception remains unabatedly coined by the dominance of spirit and the individual. A less person-related or spiritual life appears as inferior or as a precursor. This does not only pertain to plants and animals, but to our own nature as well. – A friendship with the whole nature ought to go hand in hand with befriending our own nature. Friendship is based on sympathy, commitment and a form of certain equality. However, as long as we perceive ourselves as a person only, as long as we confound the specific personal and spiritual side of humans with the entity of humans, we will only be able to maintain real friendships with persons, in other words humans. Only when we may realize that we are creatures like other creatures and things like other things, the sense of heart and sympathy can open up to the whole world and life.

I am looking forward to next wednesday.

Kind regards

R. G.

Fig. page 11: Source: https://www.oldbookillustrations.com/illustrations/androcles-lion/
Fig. page 12: Robert Josef Kozljanič
Fig. page 14: Inga Haverkampf
Fig. page 16: Antonia Kölbl
Fig. page 17: Source: https://commons.wikimedia.org/wiki/File:Bonifatius_Dona-reiche.jpg
Fig. page 21: (c) www.mantarayshawaii.com, source: youtube.com/user/Man-taRaysHawaii
Fig. page 27: Stef Sauer
Fig. page 28: Robert Josef Kozljanič
Fig. page 36: Robert Josef Kozljanič
Fig. page 37: (c) https://creativecommons.org/licenses/by-sa/2.0/de/legalcode, author Christian Bickel, source: https://commons.wikimedia.org/wiki/File:Al-fastein_1.jpg
Fig. page 40: Photographer: Armin Kübelbeck, CC-BY-SA, https://creativecom-mons.org/licenses/by-sa/3.0/legalcode, source: Wikimedia Commons https://commons.wikimedia.org/wiki/File:Nietzsche-Stein_01.jpg
Fig. page 48: Dr Peter Schomerus
Fig. page 54: Kurt Daschner
Fig. page 59: Robert Josef Kozljanič
Fig. page 64: https://commons.wikimedia.org/wiki/File:Clione_limacina_by_NOAA.jpg, author: Kevin Raskoff, Hidden Ocean 2005, Location: Alaska, Beaufort Sea, North of Point BarrowExploration, source: https://photolib.noaa.gov/Collections/Voyage/Other/emodule/1340/eitem/77215
Fig. page 74: left and right, Robert Josef Kozljanič
Fig. page 76: Robert Josef Kozljanič
Fig. page 82: Robert Josef Kozljanič
Fig. page 84: Robert Josef Kozljanič
Fig. page 90: Robert Josef Kozljanič
Fig. page 99: Robert Josef Kozljanič
Fig. page 119: Source: Archivo General de la Nacion Argentina, inventory no. 361903, https://www.facebook.com/ArchivoGeneraldelaNacionArgentina/pho-tos/a.141923792499512/1674077159284160?type=1&theater
Fig. page 131: Robert Josef Kozljanič

THE AUTHORS

RUDOLF GASSENHUBER studied philosophy, psychology and pedagogy in Regensburg. Diploma in pedagogy. After years of theory, he opened a carpentry and trade fair construction company with a partner. Seven years later, in 1986, he discovered programming for himself and founded a software company to develop a database for catalogue production, see www.gassenhuber.de. His ties to philosophy and psychology remained alive unchanged. For about ten years he has also been working as a psychotherapist and philosophical counsellor in his own practice, see www.kontingenztherapie.de

ROBERT JOSEF KOZLJANIČ is a life-philosopher. He works as a lecturer, course leader, social worker, author and publisher. Since 2005 main editor of the "Jahrbuch für Lebensphilosophie" ("Yearbook of Life-Philosophy"). He studied philosophy, psychology, anthropology, folklore, German studies at the Ludwig-Maximilians-University Munich. Doctorate in philosophy at the Technical University of Darmstadt (Prof. Dr. Gernot Böhme) on the topic of "The Spirit of a Place – Cultural History and Phenomenology of the Genius Loci" (2 vols, published 2004). Active in refugee and homeless work for 30 years. Conducted violence prevention and social competence courses for young people in the prisons Ebrach and Bernau. Freelancer at the Pedagogical Institute of the City of Munich. Founder and director of Albunea Verlag München (www.albunea.de). Scientific focus: Philosophy of life, old and new phenomenology, philosophy of space, nature and experiential education, art of living, aesthetics, cultural history. info@albunea.de

Printed by
Rotomail Italia S.p.A.
July 2024